# Olympic Mountains Fishing Guide

## Olympic National Park & Olympic Peninsula Lakes & Streams

### By Dave Shorett

ISBN: 0-9652116-0-6
Library of Congress Catalog Card Number: 96-76306

Publisher: LakeStream Publications, 200 Maynard Building, 119 1st Avenue South, Seattle, WA 98104-2533. Phone: (206) 842-9202.

Page layout: Charles B. Summers, Pacific Publication Services, P. O. Box H, South Bend, WA 98586. Phone: (360) 875-6091.

Maps: Jim Singer, 13215 118th Avenue N. E., Kirkland, WA 98034.

Printing: Paramount Graphics Inc., 11000 SW 11th, Suite 400, Beaverton, OR 97005-4112, (800) 524-6514.

# Acknowledgments

The author is grateful to Stan Jones for his many hours of advice and patience; John Meyer and Rich Olson of Olympic National Park; James Johnston, Terry Jackson, and Burt Weissbourd for their assistance; and Ted Lloyd, a great fishing partner for the last 25 years. Appreciation for the use of photographs goes to the National Park Service (designated as NPS in photo captions), Francis Caldwell, John Meyer, and Stan Jones Publications.

The author also wishes to acknowledge E. B. Webster, noted naturalist and founder/publisher of the Port Angeles newspaper. Although a printer by trade, his lifelong personal interest in nature led him to spend every available moment in the outdoors. During the early part of this century, the Olympic Peninsula became a special place where he hiked, camped, and fished as he became intimately familiar with its wildlife, plants, and rugged natural beauty.

Webster wrote several books about the Olympic Mountains, the reading of which served as inspiration for the writing of this fishing guide. In addition, the author brings some of Webster's experience to the modern reader by supplying throughout this book many of the splendid stories and

*E. B. Webster. Photo courtesy of the Clallam County Historical Museum.*

quotes from Webster's *Fishing in the Olympics*, published by the Evening News Inc., Port Angeles, Washington, 1923. In this way, it is hoped that at least some of the flavor of Webster's description of Olympic Mountain fishing is preserved.

# Table of Contents

# Introduction

> *"Size, both in the matter of lakes and streams and in fish, is not the measure of excellence. Give me the pure mountain stream, picturesque in its wild beauty; its cascades, tiny canyons and waterfalls; its light and shade, its lovely mosses, vines and ferns, all glistening from the spray; its tangled and overgrown trails; its half–submerged logs holding back foam covered pools —a clear stream of willing water icy cold and filled with mountain trout."*
> E. B. Webster, *Fishing in the Olympics*, 1923.

Any writer would be hard put to find a better way of describing the natural beauty of fishing in the Olympic Mountains which dominate the Northwesterly corner of the continental United States. E. B. Webster— publisher of the Port Angeles Newspaper and author of several books about the Olympic Peninsula—had the run of this vast area, 1400 square miles of which is now Olympic National Park. Most of the land surrounding the Park is designated National Forest and Wilderness Area bringing the total of public lands to nearly 3000 of the Olympic Peninsula's 6500 square miles. There are 500 miles of formal trails in the Park, nearly as many in the adjoining federal and state lands, and many miles of unmaintained paths.

Much of this area, especially Olympic National Park, is still largely wilderness. The mountains rise abruptly from sea level with the highest— Mt. Olympus—just under 8,000 feet, and many drop almost vertically as much as 3,000 feet. More than 50 glaciers cap the peaks.

Rainfall is very heavy during late fall, winter and often spring giving the Western Olympics the heaviest precipitation—as much as 200 inches—in the lower 48 states. Snowfall is said to sometimes exceed 500 inches near the crests. Precipitation on the southern slopes approaches these amounts, but considerably less falls on the eastern and particularly the northern Olympics.

The National Park Service estimates that a minimum of 51 lakes and possibly as many as 70 within the boundaries of the Park contain trout. In the lands surrounding the Park, trout can be found in at least 70 high mountain lakes and numerous lowland lakes. In addition, there are hundreds of miles of rivers and creeks in the Olympic Mountains which have both anadromous and resident fish populations.

When E. B. Webster fished the Olympics in the early 1900's, salmon, steelhead, sea–run cutthroat and Dolly Varden were very abundant in the rivers and creeks. However, it is widely believed that virtually no fish

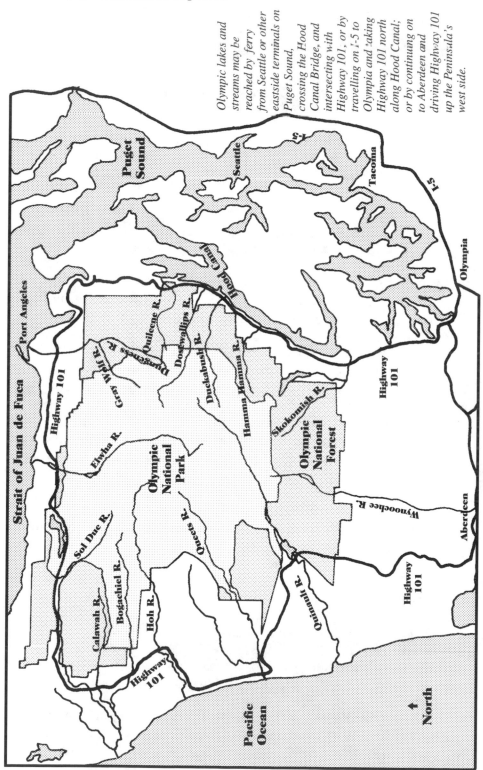

*Olympic lakes and streams may be reached by ferry from Seattle or other eastside terminals on Puget Sound, crossing the Hood Canal Bridge, and intersecting with Highway 101, or by travelling on I-5 to Olympia and taking Highway 101 north along Hood Canal; or by continuing on to Aberdeen and driving Highway 101 up the Peninsula's west side.*

existed in the high lakes and streams above the range of these sea–going fish. It is possible that in some of the upper reaches of streams, previously sea–going populations of fish were cut off from the sea by natural changes in the environment, such as stream blockage, and residualized to become residents of their streams without migrating to the sea and returning to spawn. In other streams, notably the Elwha, Wynoochee, and North Fork Skokomish, construction of dams prohibited fish from migrating out, and their progeny have existed for generations since.

Most fish now found in Olympic lakes and streams, however, are either descendants of stocked ancestors, or have been planted there by governmental agencies, private individuals, or clubs. Some time after Olympic National Park was established in 1932, a change in Park Service policy terminated its stocking programs. Thus, trout presently existing in the lakes and streams inside the Park above the reach of anadromous fish, are progeny of many generations of self–sustaining populations which successfully reproduced after stocking ceased. Outside the park, many such self-sustaining populations exist in numerous high and lowland lakes. The State of Washington, private individuals, and clubs also continue to stock many lakes and a few streams.

Webster described many a fishing trip and told many a fishing story in his books. Some of the fishing was indeed outstanding then, and some is now. But things are different today and will continue to change. Environmental degradation, in particular outdated logging and road building practices, has changed habitat in some of the lakes and streams, and affected fish populations in some instances. Siltation of streams and lakes, blockage of stream passage, and other negative impacts have changed in some locations the habitat of the fish which Webster and his contemporaries sought.

Yet, the environmental changes have not altered conditions enough that hikers and fishermen cannot continue to take many of the trips and experience the same beauty and wilderness which Webster did so long ago. If fishermen treat Olympic Mountain lakes, streams, and fish with care, there is no reason to expect anything other than the continuation of the grand experience of fishing in the Olympic Mountains.

# *How to use this book*

This guidebook is designed to give anglers, no matter what fishing technique they use, as much information as possible about fishing the Olympic Mountains. A brief section introduces Olympic stream and lake fishing for trout. The Olympic Mountain region is then discussed in four parts, North, East, South and West with a description of the streams and lakes known to hold trout, species and size of fish, and the means of access for anglers.

*Upper Elwha River rainbow trout. Author photo.*

## Olympic Trout

Trout populations are described as accurately as possible. Much more is known about fish populations of Olympic lakes than streams. The National Park Service, National Forest Service and Washington Department of Fish and Wildlife have studied most of the Olympic lakes in detail and the information provided in this book on the lakes is not merely anecdotal, it is primarily empirically based. However, lake trout populations and size vary from year to year, some lakes become barren, others previously barren are stocked (except inside the Park where stocking is a violation of federal law), species stocking policies change, and a variety of other factors affect the fish in Olympic lakes.

The Olympic rivers and creeks have been intensively studied by governmental agencies for their anadromous fish species, but less is known about resident rainbow, cutthroat, Dolly Varden, eastern brook and whitefish. The information on Olympic streams is derived from the author's experience, studies by government agencies, and discussions with numerous individuals.

Trout populations have been for the most part described conservatively, in the hope that anglers using this guide will be more often pleasantly surprised than disappointed. There are innumerable miles of fishable rivers and creeks which can be explored by the adventurous and many lakes which remain officially unnamed and obscure to fishermen.

## Access

For convenience, access to fishing each region is delineated through maps and initially, road access, then discussion of trails leading to waters not reached by road. The maps provided in this guidebook are intended to give accurate directions but are not drawn to scale. Road numbers and names, descriptions, mileage, specific hiking directions and trail mileage are as accurate as possible. However, topographic maps are indispensable in finding many of the waters described, particularly lakes, and all anglers hiking in search of trout are cautioned to use the best topographic maps and hiking guidebooks available. No one hiking off trail in search of a lake or stream should think of doing so without such maps, guidebooks, and a compass. A list of guidebooks and topographic maps is found in the appendix.

## Fishing Technique

Following the description of specific waters, an attempt is made to summarize what the author believes to be the most effective trout fishing techniques in this region. Having fished the Olympics for 40 years, beginning with bait, then spin fishing, and eventually fly fishing almost exclusively, the emphasis in this book is almost entirely on fly fishing technique. Spin fishing and fly fishing are both effective in the Olympic Mountains. Bait fishing is prohibited in most streams and many lakes but surely is the most effective of the three where it is allowed. Developing a child's interest in fishing often requires the use of bait. He or she has to catch fish to be interested. Beyond this, it is strongly recommended that fly and spin fishing be the norm. Fly fishing technique is discussed in this book because it is felt that bait fishing will soon no longer be allowed, spin fishing is rapidly being replaced among anglers by fly fishing as a preferred technique, fly fishing has the lowest impact and is most satisfying to the author.

## Useful Information

The appendices supply both necessary and helpful information which will be of assistance in having the best fishing experience possible. Regulations, hiking and fishing ethics, recommended maps and hiking guidebooks, a list of campgrounds, accommodations, addresses and phone numbers of National Park and National Forest Offices, ranger stations and State offices are all found in the appendices.

# Olympic Mountains Fishing Calendar

The following is intended as a general guide for fishing the Olympics by month and season. Regulations control the actual dates of opening and closing of fishing and vary from year to year. ALWAYS BE CERTAIN THAT REGULATIONS ALLOW FISHING.

## January, February, March.

Trout fishing is closed. Steelhead fishing is good and can be excellent. Newspapers, guides, fishing shops, sporting goods stores, resorts and fisheries biologists are all sources of information. Rain and river conditions are followed closely by these sources, as well as catch results in various rivers.

## April, May

Lowland lakes in Washington and Olympic National Park open late in April, and close late in October, with some exceptions. Stream fishing for trout opens early in June and stays open until the end of October, also with exceptions. CHECK REGULATIONS TO DETERMINE WATER OPEN TO FISHING, SPECIES, SIZE AND GEAR RESTRICTIONS.

Early season fishing is usually very good in lakes but streams are generally too high. Mills and Aldwell on the north side, Elk, Jefferson, Cushman, Price's, on the east side, Spider, Pine, Haven, Drybed lakes and Satsop lakes on the south side, and Elk and Irely on the west side all provide good early fishing.

## June

Some high lakes are accessible as trails become snow free during June. Those with good sun exposure and lower elevations become ice–free and fishable, usually with good results. Visitor centers, ranger stations and fisheries biologists are the best sources of information. Angeles, Boulder, Mink, Flapjack Lakes, Lower Lena and several others open relatively early. The more remote higher elevation lakes remain locked in ice until at least mid to late July.

Lowland lakes continue to produce well and morning and evening fly fishing become most productive. The early clearing streams, especially the small creeks and a few rivers, notably the North Fork Skokomish, Gray Wolf, Dungeness, South Fork Hoh, and Quilcene become fishable but are not at peak condition. Summer steelhead enter many streams, mainly on the west side, but in small numbers.

## July

All but the highest and most remote trails are open and by the end of the month, nearly all high lakes are clear of ice. Streams on the east and south drop into shape and fly fishing can be excellent by mid–July.

North and west side streams are generally good by late July, offering fishing for resident trout, Dolly Varden, whitefish, and a few summer steelhead, jack salmon, sea–run cutthroat, and sea–run Dolly Varden.

## August

Olympic Mountain anglers find August the best month to fish nearly all waters. All lakes are open, streams have dropped and cleared and camping is at its best. Many hike in to the Upper Elwha where there is excellent fly fishing. The upper stretches of the west side rivers are near peak fishing and anglers hike up the Queets, Hoh, Bogachiel, Calawah, both upper forks of the Quinault and remote areas of streams on all sides of the Olympics.

## September

Generally warm days and cool, often cold nights of September combine with low, clear stream conditions and ideal lake temperatures to give fishermen the kind of fishing which carries them through the winter. Trout fishing can be at its best during this month, as fish feed actively, preparing for winter.

Salmon enter streams in greater numbers on their spawning runs. They are accompanied by sea–run cutthroat and sea–run Dolly Varden.

## October

Trout fishing is fast at times but slows as lake and stream temperatures drop. Rain becomes more frequent and can make stream fishing difficult. Most mature salmon have entered or will soon enter their spawning streams and where regulations allow, salmon fishing can be very good. CHECK REGULATIONS.

## November

Trout fishing is closed in the Olympic Mountains. Winter steelhead enter the streams, gathering in estuaries first, waiting for rains to increase flow as they begin their spawning run upstream. Specific information is available from guides and sports shops. Very strict regulations govern steelhead fishing.

## December

Steelhead runs dominate the rivers and creeks and anglers pursue them both by drift boat and from shore.

> *"Back in the early nineties, when fishermen were few and trout practically unlimited in number. . . it happened that Ray Siebel, shortly after arriving at Angeles, was sitting on a log near Lake Sutherland, casting out into the ripples with a fly. Presently, a stranger came along and the two fell into a conversation.*
> *'How's the fishing?' asked the stranger.*
> *'Great' replied Ray. 'I've already caught 35 and on a fly, too.'*
> *'Perhaps you don't know me,' said the tall stranger. 'I am Jack Pike, the game warden.'*
> *' I reckon you don't know who I am, either.'*
> *'Well, who are you?' said Jack, taking out his little notebook.*
> *'I'm the damnedest liar in Clallam County,' replied Ray."*
> *—E. B. Webster*

# Fishing Olympic Mountain Lakes and Streams

## Lakes

*"When I want to enjoy an outing, a real outing, when I want to forget business, to get rid of nerves, of insomnia, I hit the trail. The trail has individuality. After one or two trips, a man becomes inti-mate with it. He longs to return to it and enter upon it."*
—E. B. Webster

Hiking into an Olympic Mountain lake is a special occasion. The scenery is always memorable and few will forget the lake, the hike, and the fishing. The color and clarity of the water varies from lake to lake, and no two lakes are in any sense identical. If one considers the overall experience, trips to Olympic Mountain lakes create lifetime memories.

Olympic Mountain lakes are so numerous that it is doubtful one could fish all of them in a lifetime. Generally, the lakes fall into three categories: 1) High lakes, such as alpine lakes and for purposes of discussion, these lakes are over 2,000 feet and always ice over during the winter, 2) Lowland lakes, under 2,000 feet which frequently have ice at times during winter, but are generally ice–free by mid–April to June, and 3) Lakes with no fish in them. While a small minority, some Olympic Mountain lakes do not have populations of trout.

### Olympic National Park Lakes

The Park Service, many years ago, converted to a natural reproduction only, no stocking program, in keeping with management plans designed to preserve the Park as the most natural ecosystem possible. As a result, those lakes within the Park that do not have reproducing trout populations do not contain trout.

Lakes which now have populations of fish and will continue to produce them, include those containing eastern brook and those with sizable inlet or outlet streams which do not dry up in summer, providing spawning habitat for rainbow and cutthroat.( Except for suspected cutthroat–rainbow hybrids existing in Lower Three Horse Lake, and native cutthroat in Irely Lake, none of the Park lakes historically contained cutthroat). Rainbow and cutthroat, believed to be capable only in rare circumstances of successfully spawning in alluvial fans, upwellings and other unique habitat within lakes, are dependent upon such streams to be self–sustaining. Eastern brook, in contrast, spawn in streams in the fall just before winter rains begin, which allows their eggs and progeny to carry over to spring and populate lakes; they are also readily capable of spawning within the perimeter habitat of the lake itself and are seldom dependent upon a stream flow for reproduction. Increasingly, the trout population in the Olympic lakes, especially in the Park, is becoming an eastern brook trout population. All of the brook trout lakes provide good fishing experiences, many of them, excellent. There remain plenty of rainbow and at least two cutthroat lakes to fish, and these will continue to provide good fishing.

## High lakes Outside Olympic National Park

Most lowland and high lakes within the Olympic Mountains outside Park boundaries continue to be stocked by the State of Washington, individuals, or fishing clubs Some have naturally reproducing populations and there will always be fish in these lakes.

Management policies for Olympic Mountain lakes outside the Park are based largely on a very instructive 1972–73 High Lake Management study done by James Johnston for the Washington Department of Fish and Wildlife, in which he surveyed all high lakes in Olympic National Forest. His study and recommendations changed high lake stocking policies dramatically. An understanding of this extensive examination is highly beneficial to any angler.

*Olympic Peninsula mountain lake. NPS photo.*

Johnston found that only 11% of the lakes in Olympic National Forest had successful reproduction for cutthroat and rainbow. Continued existence of these species in the rest of the lakes depended upon stocking policies. Nearly all lakes containing eastern brook had successful reproduction.

Two polices controlled high lake management in the Olympic National Forest at the time. First, easily accessible lakes were managed by planting large numbers of fish at close intervals, the theory being that annual natural mortalities and very high fishing pressure required this to provide good fishing. Second, lakes considerably more difficult to reach were planted less frequently, but with even higher numbers of fish, in the belief that fish planted by fixed wing aircraft had a high mortality rate and sometimes the drop would partially miss the lake. Basically, the then existing high lake management policies resembled those for the lowland lakes at that time; increasing the numbers of fish and thus the yield in numbers at the expense of allowing lakes to produce large fish, but in limited numbers. It was apparent that by continuing to stock large numbers over and over again, the size of the fish would continue to decrease and the food supply in the lake would steadily decline.

Johnston saw the food supply in the lake as a "food bank." By stocking lakes with appropriate numbers of fish to live off the annual production of this food bank, without invading the "principal," a lake could sustain the maximum fish pounds per acre it was capable of producing. Several studies supported this finding, most of which were based upon the introduction of large numbers of fish into lakes and subsequently finding a dramatic decrease in the invertebrate and insect populations, essentially the food supply of the lake. This process is described as "over cropping." Johnston also found that fish which are simply maintaining themselves, usually skinny and stunted, tend to live longer than their fatter, healthier counterparts. He felt that even one initial overstocking of a lake could keep a lake from producing quality size fish for as long as 10 years, even in the absence of natural reproduction. Remarkably, a study in 1964 found rainbow trout still in a lake 11 years after planting and 14 year–old rainbow in Klone Lake #1.

In contrast, if a lake were stocked with numbers less than the maximum population sustainable by its "food bank," it was found that the fish grew very fast and at almost double the poundage compared to overstock situations. Further, Johnston discovered that natural mortalities in high lakes seem to be lower than in lowland lakes.

He then studied the carrying capacity of each lake and determined how each should be stocked, ranking the major lakes of the Olympic National Forest in order of their productive capacities. Carrying capacity, availability or non-availability of reproduction, combined with estimated fishing pressure then determined stocking policies, along with the overall decision to plant rainbow and cutthroat, but no more eastern brook.

The final conclusion which Johnston reached was the majority of the lakes should be planted at 50% of maximum numbers of fish that are allowable for sustained production and the lakes restocked every 4 or 5 years. This seems to be essentially the policy which is followed with high lakes in Olympic National Forest and there is no doubt that it has dramatically improved fishing in most of them.

# *Streams*

*"A day on a mountain stream; a couple of hours spent enticing 7 to 10 inch trout from their hiding places under rock ledges, beneath the foamy scum of tiny pools, or from the shadow of some great log or root. . . ."—E. B. Webster*

## Trout

Stream fishing for trout in the Olympic Mountains is generally best in the upper stretches of the rivers and creeks. The lower sections of almost all Olympic streams are the primary habitat of anadromous fish—steelhead, salmon, sea–run cutthroat, and sea–run Dolly Varden. Olympic resident trout do not thrive in competition with anadromous fry and smolts and it is rare to find sizable trout in this part of the stream. Some steelhead smolts will reach 12-14 inches in the lower sections and sometimes further upstream and make for exciting fishing, but they are few in number. Getting toward upper reaches and above the habitat of anadromous species is normally essential to finding good trout fishing. In turn, this requires driving a distance up the road off the main highway and in the majority of cases, fishing upstream, either by wading the river or creek, hiking by trail, or bushwhacking.

*Olympic Peninsula mountain stream. Author photo.*

## Salmon, Steelhead, Sea-Run Cutthroat, and Sea-Run Dolly Varden

Salmon fishing in Olympic rivers begins in spring, slows in summer and picks up in fall and winter. The large coastal rivers such as the Queets, Hoh, Bogachiel, Humptulips, Quinault, Sol Duc and a few others are far more productive for salmon than the east and south side rivers, with a few exceptions such as the Wynoochee and Satsop on the south side.

Historically, some of the world's finest steelhead fishing has been available on the Olympic Peninsula in most of the rivers which are productive for salmon, but runs have seriously declined over time. Just about all Olympic rivers and most of the bigger creeks support steelhead populations, and experienced fishermen know where to look and when. Winter run steelhead are more numerous on the Peninsula, but there are small runs of summer run steelhead, which, if you can find them, will take a nymph, wet fly, streamer, and even a dry fly once in awhile, adding a real thrill to a day of fishing for trout. Summer run steelhead locations and secrets are heavily guarded by those who know them. Asking around at the usual sources may help novice fisherman, but expect to encounter heavy doses of lying. All wild steelhead must be released.

Sea–run cutthroat and sea–run Dolly Varden, at one time very abundant in Olympic rivers and creeks, usually enter the streams with salmon in the fall, spawning on their own cycles. Sea–run cutthroat have been known to grow to well over 20 inches, but most are 12–16 inches when caught in the Olympics. Called harvest trout by some, because they are found in good numbers in the fall at harvest time, sea–run cutthroat are particular favorites of fly fishermen because they will rise readily to a dry fly, are not picky and can be caught below the surface without too much difficulty if they are not in the mood to rise. Long time Olympic fishermen still savor the "old days" when it seemed nearly every hole held plenty of sea–runs in the fall.

There has been a drastic decline in the number of sea–run cutthroat on the Olympic Peninsula and the various fishery agencies are not in agreement about the causes. These cutthroat can still be found and fished for but it often takes luck, a lot of exploration, a good guide, a long float, lots of patience and most often all combined to get in a really good day of sea–run cutthroat fishing. Experienced anglers who know the rivers and creeks from fishing during sea–run time for years are the best source of information but not likely to give away any secrets. Even if regulations don't require it, all sea–run cutthroat should be released.

Sea–run Dolly Varden also provide some sport for fly fishermen but are much more limited in numbers and the streams they enter. Because of their carnivorous feeding habits, they are far more reluctant to rise to a fly, and must nearly always be fished with a streamer or nymph. Dollies can get quite large and fish over 20 inches are not unusual. On the Olympic Penin-sula, all Dolly Varden/Bull Trout must be released.

The amount of information on location, access and technique for success in catching salmon, steelhead, sea–run cutthroat and sea–run Dolly Varden is far beyond the scope of this book and can be found in several other books. Information on where, when, and how to fish for these species is best obtained from guides, local sports shops, fisheries agencies and hatcheries.

All of these anadromous species have declined in Olympic streams to the point where it is the author's opinion that strict catch and release must be practiced by all anglers, even when regulations don't require it.

*Queets River fishermen. Stan Jones photo.*

# Northern Olympics

## Dungeness

### Dungeness River

> *"The Dungeness was a great fishing stream in those days. It was two miles upriver to this opening and the ice on the river was fully a foot thick....yet the whole bed of the river was for two miles so packed with trout that the heavy covering of tough ice in places rolled and tossed like the waves of the sea. The first arrival of the fish at the open hole was marked with a geyser–like eruption of trout, twenty feet across and about seven feet high... the air was filled with a murmuring sound that could be heard quite down to Old Town, while some of the residents claimed their houses trembled as with a continued earthquake." —Charles Stakemiller from Fishing in the Olympics, by E.B. Webster*

The Dungeness is an anadromous fish river for much of its length, but above the confluence with the Gray Wolf river seems to support very few salmon or steelhead, with the result that it is packed with trout. It is a relatively high gradient river, with lots of pocket water and very few slow runs.

Trout fishing is consistent along the Dungeness above its junction with the Gray Wolf for 7–10 inch fish. Once the river seasonally settles down to its smallest size, it is much easier to fish the pockets and holes, but it is not terribly difficult to catch fish anytime the river is clear, even if high.

Fishing access for trout is first available at the Dungeness Forks Campground, 7.6 miles off Highway 101 up the Palo Alto Road, leading to the Dungeness trails. Here, the river is medium size, bigger than the Quilcene but smaller than the Hamma Hamma. The Gray Wolf joins the Dungeness at the campground. A rough trail follows the river downstream, where there is a brief fishable stretch before the river enters a steep canyon. Dolly Varden inhabit this stretch and some will rise to a dry fly. There are small rainbow as well. The largest trout one is likely to encounter is about 12 inches, unless there is a surprise, usually from a Dolly.

The next good access point is up the road at East Crossing Campground.

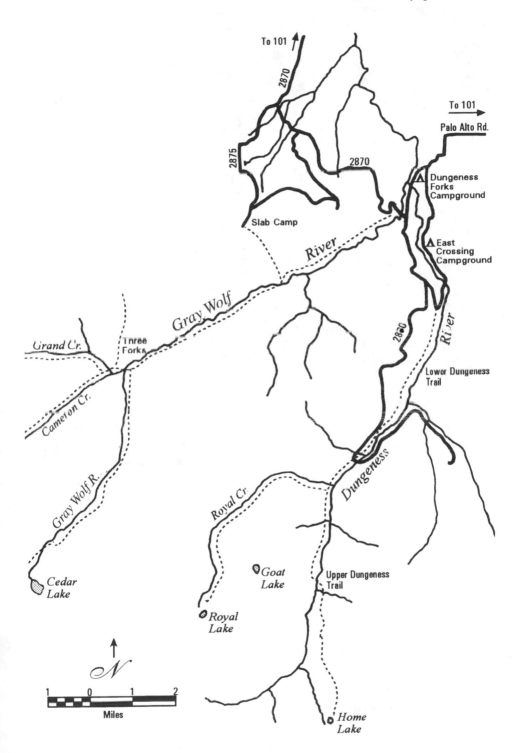

*Upper Dungeness River.  Francis Caldwell photo.*

Several miles of access to the river are also available by hiking the Lower Dungeness Trail, beginning l2.6 miles in from Highway 101. The trailhead is hidden off to the left of the road, a few hundreds yards uphill from the bridge crossing the river at Goldcreek Shelter. From East Crossing to the end of the Lower Dungeness Trail, the river flattens a bit, is easily fished and there is an abundant population of trout, with quite a few in the 10–11 inch range.

At the end of the Dungeness Road, 17.4 long dusty miles from Highway 101, there is a large parking lot where the Upper Dungeness Trail begins. There is fair fishing up and down the river from the parking lot and there are rough fishermen's trails on both sides leading upstream. The river, as might be expected, continues to get smaller, clears earlier and is more easily fished, particularly in the slower runs which are found in the occasional flatter areas of the river, usually running a couple hundred yards before the plunge pool character of the river takes over again.

The river in this area is essentially a large creek about a cast across, with lots of small holes, but also plenty of shallow boulder water. It requires some walking to get from plunge pool to plunge pool. Some of the pools are almost chest deep and hold decent fish; 8 and 9 inch rainbow are common in this part of the Dungeness and there are also Dolly Varden, some of which ascend to a dry fly. Dollies grow as large as 13–14 inches in this section of the river and a rare lunker rainbow to 11–13 inches. The fish tend to be fat and energetic.

The road to the Tubal Cain Trail, which begins at the parking lot borders the river about a mile downstream and there is good access. Downstream from this point, the river drops deep into a canyon and is accessible only through pioneer work.

## Goat Lake (5980)

Locating Goat Lake and then reaching it is indisputably a challenge and can be dangerous. Hike the upper Dungeness River Trail 1 mile to the junction with Rail Creek Trail then another approximately 2 miles to Camp Handy, at 3100 feet, where the river must be forded. The trail to Goat Lake, such as it is, travels uphill, gaining 2800 feet of elevation in less than 2 miles to reach the lake. Goat Lake is one of the highest lakes on the Olympic Peninsula. This is an extremely arduous hike, requires map and compass and certainly is not a day trip.

The 8 acre lake is approximately 25 feet deep and contains abundant fresh water shrimp. When rainbow trout were initially planted in 1971 by the Trailblazers, they grew extremely fast, in one year to a fat average 11 inch size. Surveys in 1973 determined the trout to be an average at age two of 16 inches and 2 pounds, one 19 inch, 3 pounder was found.

The Forest Service long ago expressed concern about damage to the lake from too many visits by fishermen, suggested that it be checked for 4 years and, if very little damage occurred, it be restocked every 4 years. Records show it has been planted every 4 years with rainbow. As long as this is the case, the probability is for excellent rainbow fishing.

## Royal Lake (5100)

A 2 acre lake containing eastern brook, Royal Lake is reached by an 8 mile long trail beginning at the Upper Dungeness Trail and gaining 2900 feet.

## Home Lake (5350)

An approximately one acre lake at the headwaters of the Dungeness River, Home Lake is 9.7 miles from the Upper Dungeness trailhead. Seldom visited, it contains eastern brook.

## Buckhorn Lake (See Quilcene)

## Gray Wolf River

It has been reported in several places that one, if not the last, refuge of the Gray Wolf which roamed the Olympic Mountains, was the valley through which this beautiful river flows. The Gray Wolf is medium sized, fast flowing and joins with the upper Dungeness to form the main stem of the Dungeness River. Because it is not glacially fed, it is one of the first Olympic rivers to clear and can be fished early.

The river is found by driving road #2880 beyond Dungeness Forks Campground, turning right on road #2870 and crossing a bridge over the Gray Wolf. Immediately beyond the bridge is the Lower Gray Wolf trailhead. The trail travels away from the river uphill and then descends in 2 miles to meet the Gray Wolf. The river is fishable at this point and gets a lot of pressure, both upstream and downstream.

The trail continues upriver, ascending and descending, meeting the river in about 1.5 miles, climbs again, comes down to river again and crosses it. Eventually, approximately 5.5 miles up the river, the trail is intersected by the Slab Camp Trail which runs out to a road in 2.5 miles, an approximately 1000 ft. elevation gain.

A nice one–way hike and fishing trip can be accomplished by parking one car at the lower Gray Wolf Trailhead, driving to the Slab Camp trailhead, approximately 9 road miles, and spending the day hiking and fishing downstream and out at the lower Gray Wolf trailhead. The total hike is about 8 miles, the first 2.5 miles downhill from the Slab Camp trailhead.

The Gray Wolf is readily wadeable, predominately pocket water, but also has some very deep pools with long tail outs. Fishing is good in the area where the Slab Camp Trail meets the river, primarily because of the presence of Dolly Varden to 15–18 inches. The Dollies in the deep holes stubbornly resist rising to a dry fly, but they are also found in pocket water in the Gray Wolf and even in areas as shallow as 2 feet deep at times. Surprisingly, the Dollies here will rise to a dry fly, fight and jump and are very substantial fish indeed. An effective fly is an Elk Hair Caddis, size 12.

If they won't take dry flies, try the traditional Dolly technique, fishing deep with wet flies and bait imitation type flies such as muddler minnows and woolly buggers. The Dollies provide a genuine "big fish" experience and though they still aren't as willing as the small rainbow in the Gray Wolf to rise to a dry fly, the combination of the small 7–10 inch rainbow with the rare 12 incher, and the possibility of hooking an occasional Dolly can make this gratifying fishing.

In odd numbered years, pink salmon, "humpies," return in substantial numbers and make fishing for rainbow and Dollies more difficult, because the Dollies in particular, have humpie spawn on their minds. The humpies don't get into the river though until August, at the earliest, and generally later in the month.

There are several campsites along the river both upstream and downstream and this need not be a day trip.

The Gray Wolf Trail continues upriver from the Slab Camp Trail intersection, but mostly too far above the river for good access until it descends

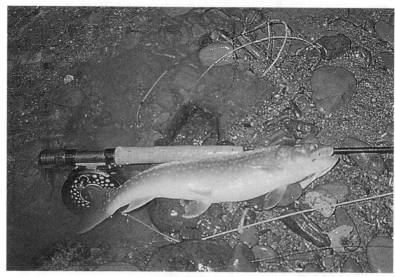

*Gray Wolf River Dolly Varden. Author photo.*

at 9.8 miles to meet the Cameron Creek Trail, which begins at Three Forks, reached by hiking down from Deer Park, a 4.5 mile descent of 3400 feet.

The upper Gray Wolf is a clear, beautiful, creek–size stream filled with small trout. Grand Creek, Cameron Creek and the upper Gray Wolf join at Three Forks to form the mainstem Gray Wolf River. This is a popular fishing spot, allowing not only access to three different streams, but also good fishing at the juncture and downstream. There are rainbow, Dolly Varden and eastern brook in all three streams and there have been reports of very large eastern brook in Grand Creek. There are several possible one–way hiking and fishing trips through this area, all requiring two vehicles, left at Slab Camp trailhead, Deer Park, or Obstruction Point.

# Deer Park

Deer Park provides the nearest entry point for anglers to the upper Gray Wolf River, Grand Creek, Cameron Creek and Cedar Lake.

## Upper Gray Wolf River, Grand Creek, Cameron Creek, Three Forks (see Dungeness)

## Cedar Lake (5280)

A 21 acre lake, historically stocked with rainbow believed to have reproduced through utilizing sufficient spawning habitat, Cedar is known as a productive lake for fishing for good sized rainbow to 15 inches. The shortest route is off the upper Gray Wolf Trail through a well–developed 3 mile, 1380 foot elevation gain trail beginning at Fall's Shelter, at mile 5.4 on the upper Gray Wolf Trail.

# Heart o' the Hills

## Lake Angeles (4196)

At Heart o' the Hills a 3.5 mile trail gains a well–traveled 2400 feet to reach Lake Angeles, 20 acres, 30 feet deep. Despite being heavily fished, the lake is profoundly packed with fat, 8–10 inch eastern brook. Set deep in a cirque, it is difficult to fish from shore and a raft is very useful. This is a good hike with children and keeping brookies to eat from the lake will only help diminish the over–abundant trout population here.

# Obstruction Point

## P. J. Lake (4500), Grand Lake (4740), Moose Lake (5075) and Gladys Lake (5400)

At the end of Obstruction Point Road is the trailhead to a number of ponds which are said to have trout, and three lakes, Grand, Moose and

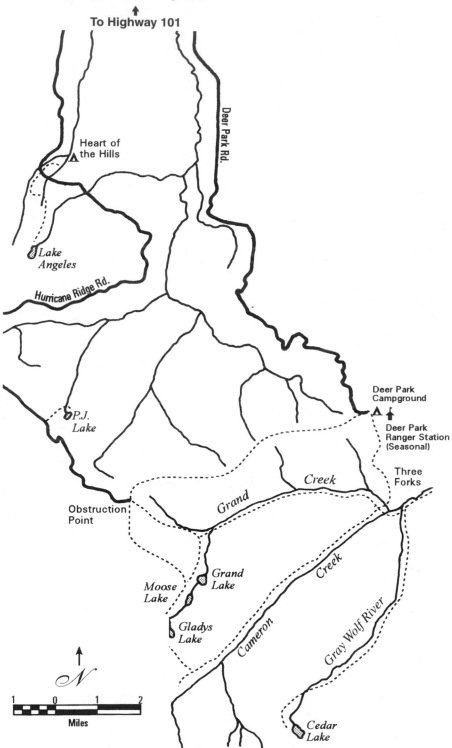

To Highway 101

Deer Park Rd.

Heart of the Hills

Lake Angeles

Hurricane Ridge Rd.

P.J. Lake

Deer Park Campground

Deer Park Ranger Station (Seasonal)

Three Forks

*Creek*

*Grand*

Obstruction Point

Grand Lake

Moose Lake

*Creek*

Gladys Lake

*Cameron*

*Gray Wolf River*

N

|  1    0    1    2  |
| Miles |

Cedar Lake

Gladys. Before reaching the end of the Obstruction Point Road, at 3.8 miles near an abandoned campground, a trail descends sharply 0.9 miles, 500 feet to P. J. Lake, allegedly named for an early jeweler from Port Angeles who fished it so often that other anglers gave it this title. The lake lies in a cirque, is approximately 1 acre and nearly 30 feet deep. It has a very large population of brookies to 10 inches.

The trail to Grand, Moose and Gladys lakes begins at Grand Ridge trailhead at the end of Obstruction Point road. Camping restrictions may apply to this area and should be checked with the Park Service. Grand Lake is reached with an elevation drop of 1300 feet at 4.3 miles or, alternatively, a shorter route starting from Grand Pass Trail, beginning also at Obstruction Point. Within 3.8 miles this trail reaches Grand Lake and in another 0.5 miles, Moose Lake, which is so named, not because of the presence of moose, but after a local hunter, Frank Moose. (There have never been any moose in the Olympics). Continuing uphill, in 0.7 miles, the hiker arrives at Gladys Lake.

All three lakes contain abundant eastern brook, 8–10 inches and Grand also has a small number of rainbow. Grand is 13 acres, Gladys 6 acres, and Moose 7 acres. Gladys is said to be named for the wife of a deputy sheriff in Clallam County who first introduced trout to this lake.

# Elwha

## Aldwell Lake (250)

A 320 acre reservoir formed by a dam on the lower Elwha River, Aldwell has eastern brook, rainbow, and kokanee. The inlet area next to the campground and upstream occasionally provides good fishing.

If the proposed removal of dams on the Elwha ever occurs, Aldwell Lake will cease to exist, along with Lake Mills.

## Little River

The Little River Road begins approximately 0.25 miles above Highway 101 on the Elwha Road. Little River is also known as the Too Little River locally because it simply isn't

*Elwha River. NPS photo.*

big enough to hold fish of any size. It is fairly easy to wade, and casting is not impossible but the distance between holding water is discouragingly long.

## Lower Elwha River

Continuing up the Elwha Road beyond Little River, there are about 5 miles of fishable water on the Elwha River between Lake Aldwell and Lake Mills. Most of the river is easily accessible from the road and there is also a trail on the west side of the river beginning in Altair Campground. This section of the Elwha looks great, but the fishing doesn't really measure up. Although there are always rumors of the occasional 14 inch rainbow, mostly what one finds is numerous small fish in pockets, ranging to about 9 inches. Still, once the river drops to a wadeable size and the color clears, it is an enjoyable stretch of lovely water on which to spend an afternoon or evening casting a line. Special regulations govern fishing in this section of the Elwha and current restrictions should be checked.

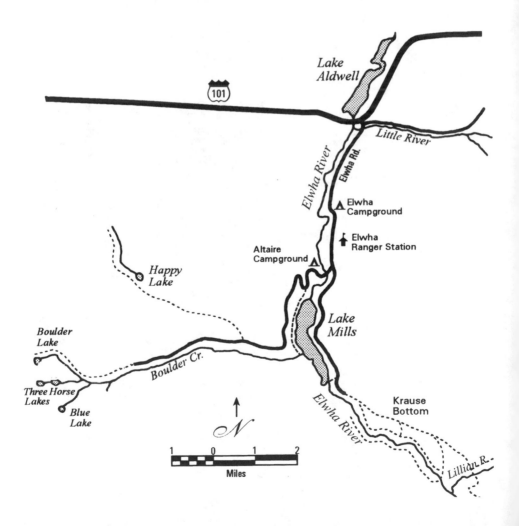

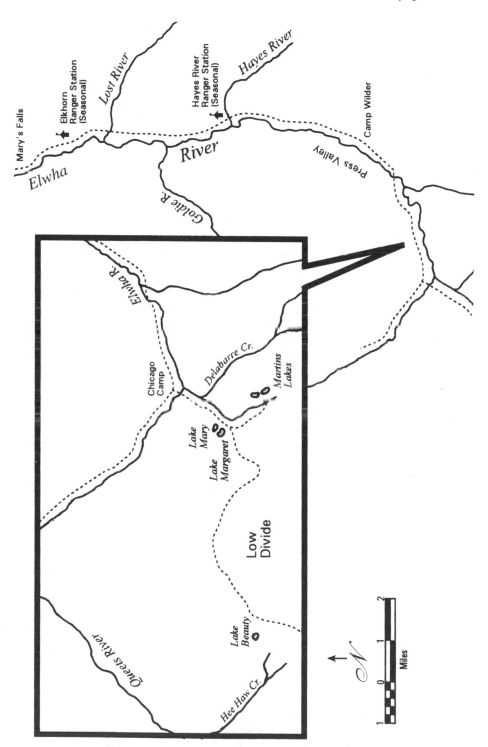

# Lake Mills (600)

The Elwha road eventually reaches Lake Mills, the upper impoundment of the Elwha. There is a public boat launch at the lower west end, and a trail which extends 2 miles up the lake's west side to Boulder Creek. Boat fishing is the best way to go at Lake Mills, but careful attention and caution are advised because the lake is subject to strong winds dangerous to small boats. This is a 451 acre lake with special regulations, producing eastern brook, Dolly Varden, cutthroat and rainbow. Fishing can be very good here for knowledgeable anglers.

## Upper Elwha River

The Elwha Road ends just beyond Lake Mills, at Whiskey Bend and here the Elwha Trail begins. At 1.2 miles, a branch trail leads a steep 0.5 miles down to Rica Canyon and the first really fishable spot in the upper Elwha. This area is heavily fished and is not as productive as the river further up. Nonetheless, the Rica Canyon Trail can be followed close to the river for approximately a mile, at which point the trail goes uphill and then returns again to the river, leaves again and returns yet again in Krause Bottom where there are numerous campsites. The river then enters a canyon and anglers must return to the main trail and either hike to the upper reaches of the Elwha or return to the trailhead.

The upper Elwha is well known for its excellent fishing for rainbow to 18–20 inches and some monster Dolly Varden in the deep holes: E. B. Webster observed:

> "... inasmuch as the Rainbow is the fightingest fish of all the trout family, and as the Elwha drains all the north central part of the Olympics, we have here a combination which the man in search of an ideal outing can find nowhere in the country....(the rainbow) here grows to a truly immense size, specimens eighteen and twenty inches in length being, if not very common, at least sufficiently so that one would never think of packing them very far for the pleasure of exhibiting them to friends."

To reach the upper river, bypass the opportunity to fish Rica Canyon and Krause Bottom and continue on the trail, which travels well above the Elwha to cross the Lillian River at 4.6 miles, elevation gain approximately 300 feet. For those who wish to try fishing the Lillian's upper stretches, there is a trail which travels upstream above it approximately 2.3 miles. This trail starts slightly more than 0.5 miles before the Elwha Trail crosses the Lillian, dead–ending on the upper portion of this river in a flatter section.

The Lillian, no more than a 3/4 cast across, is fast, pocket water, in one of the darkest wooded areas one would ever fish, the sun almost never penetrating the dense cover. Fishable from both upstream and downstream from the bridge where it is crossed by the Elwha Trail, it has beautifully

*Upper Elwha River campsite. Author photo.*

colored rainbow to 10 inches. Any trout caught in this section of the river should be carefully handled and released.

Fishing on the upper Elwha is not really possible until Mary's Falls, 9.7 miles from the beginning of the Elwha Trail. The next 8.5 miles to the Hayes River Ranger Station provide plenty of good fishing. The trail then forks at the ranger station, the left branch heading for Hayden Pass and the Dosewallips River, the right fork continuing on up the Elwha and out over the Low Divide to the Quinault River.

If you are willing to walk a 9.7 mile half–day hike in, you can find excellent fishing in the Upper Elwha which will keep you busy as long as you want. Most dedicated anglers camp further in, and fish up the river, some as part of a cross–Olympic hike, fishing the Elwha to the Low Divide, crossing, and fishing the Quinault on out to its trailhead on the West side of the Olympics.

Approximately 13 miles in, Lost River is crossed. This is a sizable river with rainbow. At 16.5 miles, Hayes River enters the Elwha and it, too, has excellent fishing with trout to 14 inches.

Continuing on the Elwha Trail past the Hayes Ranger Station, hikers travel through Press Valley and miles of good fishing on the now smaller Elwha, eventually to Lake Margaret (3600) and Lake Mary (3350) located at the Low Divide. Lake Margaret is 6 acres, has no fish and Lake Mary is a 3 acre eastern brook lake.

Also at the Low Divide and then off 0.3 miles, at the head of Hee Haw Creek is Lake Beauty (4770), 3 acres. It is unknown if the lake contains fish.

From the Low Divide another trail leads 2.4 miles to Martin's Lakes (4650) the upper of which is 3 acres and the lower 2 acres. It is not known whether these lakes contain trout.

# Boulder Creek

The Boulder Creek Road, also known as the Olympic Hot Springs Road, begins at the north end of Lake Mills and ends approximately 1 mile from Boulder Creek Campground.

## Boulder Creek.

From the boat launch on the west side of Lake Mills, hike 2 miles, fishing along Lake Mills as you like, to the mouth of Boulder Creek. The stream produces small trout.

## Happy Lake (4875)

The Happy Ridge Trail begins on the right side of Boulder Creek Road approximately 1 mile before the road end. Hike 4.5 miles to the branch trail to Happy lake. The elevation gain is 3700 feet, losing 600 feet in the last 0.5 miles descent to this shallow 3 acre lake, which is undergoing eutrophication. There is presently no information regarding the existence of trout in the lake, but it has been reported to hold eastern brook.

The Boulder Creek Road used to end at the campground, but because of heavy use of the few remaining hot spring pools, the Park Service blocked off the road a mile before the campground, so that people would have to walk at least that distance to reach the springs and campground. Several trails lead from the campground to lakes.

The Boulder Creek Campground is at the site of the former Olympic Hot Springs Resort, which at one time could only be reached by a 10 mile hike:

> *"Hung on a narrow shelf on the mountainside, over a canyon threaded by the roaring Boulder in its express train speed to the Elwha and the sea, the hotel presently comes into view. A hundred foot high bridge is to be crossed before one reaches the hotel, the bath houses, the open air pools and rows of tents and tent–houses where comfortable beds and abundant fresh air ensure a night of deep, unbroken slumber." —E. B. Webster*

A road was later built to the resort and a cab could be hired in Port Angeles to make the trip. The resort burned down in 1940, was revived for a time by the Park Service and the area later allowed to return to its natural state.

## Boulder Lake (4350)

The Boulder Lake Trail begins 0.6 miles west of Boulder Creek Campground on Appleton Pass Trail. 2.8 miles later and 2,000 feet higher popular Boulder Lake is reached. It is 8 acres and contains eastern brook.

## Lower Three Horse Lake (4100) and Upper Three Horse Lake (4300)

Approximately half–way up Boulder Lake Trail, to the southwest, lie Lower Three Horse and Upper Three Horse, both 3 acres, situated at the end of a steep canyon. The lower lake has reproducing rainbow and West Slope

*Three Horse Lake. John Meyer photo.*

cutthroat. Reaching these lakes requires a cross–country hike via a way trail beginning at the east shore of Boulder Lake, near its outlet contouring southerly at or below 4500 feet. Map and compass required.

## Blue Lake (4800)

South, and slightly east of lower Three Horse Lake, approximately 1 mile, is Blue Lake, 2 acres, which is believed to have eastern brook. Careful map and compass work is required.

# Lake Crescent

## Barnes Creek

This sizable creek flows into Lake Crescent at the side of Crescent Lodge. There is a trail up the creek from the lodge and also from Marymere Falls Trail parking lot. Early in the season the creek is worth fishing. It has good numbers of cutthroat to 12 inches in the holes and a few small rainbow. The cutthroat inhabit slow moving and almost still waters of holes and rainbow tend to be smaller and in slightly faster water. This is "drop it in the hole, hook one, maybe two fish, and move on" water.

Up the creek 0.5 miles, the crowds depart on their way to Marymere Falls and the trail continues up the creek, but it becomes smaller, even brushier than before and access is very difficult. Climbing over large moss covered logs and fighting through Devil's Club to reach small holes seem to be worth it after a winter waiting to fish for trout, but just barely. The cutthroat are dark and profusely spotted, leading one to suspect that they are a strain unique to this creek. If time allows, hike in about 2–3 miles to the canyon area below Mt. Storm King, where the creek deepens in places and holds more sizable rainbow, cutthroat, and a few eastern brook.

# Eagle Lakes

There are three small lakes, 1.5, 0.75 and 0.5 acres located at 3200 feet, 2800 feet, and 2500 feet respectively. Hike up Aurora Ridge Trail 5.6 miles, a 2550 foot elevation gain, then 0.6 miles to Eagle Lakes. The largest of these lakes is known to hold very substantial numbers of brook trout to 12 inches.

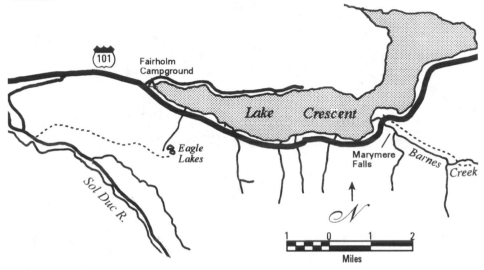

# Lake Crescent

Lake Crescent provides a unique fishery. It contains two unusual strains of trout, the Crescenti and the Beardslee. The Beardslee exist in the teens and are extremely difficult to locate and catch because there are not great numbers in this very large lake. A real challenge does exist, however, nearly unmatched anywhere else in Washington. Anglers try for Lake Crescent trout with heavy sinkers and spoons and they are nearly always taken deep. Inventive fly fishermen might develop their own style of catching these extraordinary fish.

*Lake Crescent Beardslee Trout. NPS photo.*

E.B. Webster, in 1923, said of Lake Crescent fishing:

> *"The hardest fighting fish, the gamest fish in all the world is the Lake Crescent Beardslee. Apparently a Beardslee is traveling at the rate of 25 mph when he strikes. He will break water 7 feet high , more or less, and sometimes as often as 7 or 8 times. At the present time, Beardslees are caught on a silver spoon, handmade. They cost $3.00, are made in Seattle. ...landing the ordinary l5 or l6 pound Beardslee requires a half hour to an hour...but frequently a big one will fight a full two hours before being brought to net."*

In support of his claim, Webster tells the following story:

> *". . . rowing slowly past Beardslee Point when Hine had a strike that nearly lifted him from his seat. In spite of the click, the emergency brake and the duhicky, and in spite of the fact that Potter had started the engine and was making something like 25 knots an hour, the line began to smoke, the reel bearings melted, and presently the rod caught on fire. A second later there was an explosion, burning gas sprayed the boat and covered the lake; both Hine and Potter took a headlong dive and it was with the greatest difficulty they managed to get beyond the zone of blazing water, where they were picked up by another skiff."*

# Sol Duc

## Sol Duc River

The Sol Duc is an almost entirely anadromous fish river and quite famous for that, but not much known for trout fishing. There is plenty of access to the Sol Duc where Highway 101 crosses it after it flows out of the Park toward its eventual confluence near Forks with the Bogachiel River. In its lowest stretches, the Sol Duc is one of the most beautiful rivers anywhere and supports large runs of anadromous fish, including a sizable population of sea–run cutthroat.

It is 10.9 road miles from Highway 101 to Sol Duc Hot Springs and another l.7 miles to the road end. Frequent access to the river is possible down a steep bank to the river after driving a couple of miles up the road.

The North Fork flows in 8 miles up the road. It is a rather small tributary and there is a trail which roughly follows it for about 5 miles. It contains small trout and its upper reaches are seldom fished.

Below the North Fork, during the summer the Sol Duc becomes a nice, fishable size, but has a population of disappointingly small trout. Above its confluence with the North Fork, the river is as much creek as it is river, full in the spring and quite small in the fall. Still, the anadromous fish do penetrate far up this stretch of the river.

In low water, fishing the Sol Duc above the North Fork is mainly boulder hopping, fishing to small pools. The pools are still deep, but this is very difficult going because the rocks are slippery and there is little good

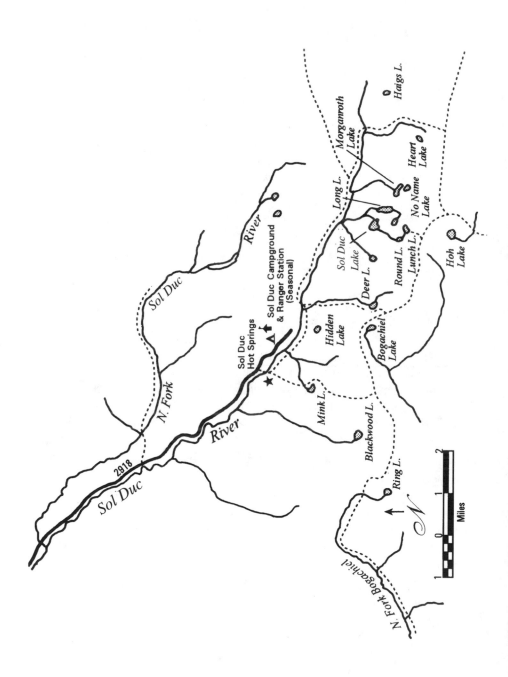

footing. This is an easy place to fall in. There are so many fry in the river that one's dry fly gets knocked down constantly.

Above the hot springs and the campground the river flattens and small rainbow abound, along with a few cutthroat. These trout rise very willingly to a dry fly. There are said to be eastern brook below Sol Duc Falls, 0.7 miles by trail above the campground.

Trout fishing is difficult in this beautiful river and there seem to be no resident trout above Sol Duc Falls where there would be no competition from anadromous fish. An interesting side note is that E. B. Webster describes the discovery of a Dolly Varden type fish above Sol Duc Falls. They were found there, "mature, filled with eggs at four inches." Theoretically, his discovery preceded planting of any eastern brook anywhere in Olympic National Park. Webster called this trout the "Alpine Trout." He sent specimens preserved in formaldehyde to a fisheries biologist in New York, who disappointingly, declared them to be eastern brook. Webster has been vindicated by Park Service electro–shock surveys, which found numerous Dolly Varden and one brook trout above the Falls.

# Sol Duc: Mink Lake Trail

The Mink Lake Trail, which begins at Sol Duc Hot Springs Resort, leads to several lakes.

## Mink Lake (3080)

Located in a heavily wooded valley, reached 2.5 miles in from the trailhead at Sol Duc Hot Springs, a 1400 foot elevation gain, popular Mink Lake is 10 acres and contains eastern brook. As with most eastern brook lakes, Mink really cannot be over fished and it has been observed that sustained fishing pressure may account for the respectable size of the brookies in this lake. It is undergoing eutrophication and difficult to fish.

## Blackwood Lake (3000)

Blackwood Lake is reached by cross–country hiking after following the Mink Lake Trail 5.4 miles, then heading west another approximately 1.5 miles, and up a steep half-mile ascent, then descent to the lake, elevation gain 1300 feet. It may also be found by following its outlet creek from the Sol Duc resort area. Map and compass work are necessary. Infrequently fished, this 16 acre lake contains eastern brook.

## Ring Lake (2900)

Ring Lake is approximately 1.5 miles uphill from the 21 Mile Shelter on the Bogachiel Trail, but is in fact considerably closer, but a lot steeper hike when approached from the Mink Lake Trail, about 11 miles from the Mink Lake trailhead, then cross–country uphill about 1000 feet to the lake. It is 2 acres and holds rainbow, which are able to spawn to a limited extent. Some very large trout have been caught in this shallow and easy to fish lake.

# Sol Duc: Deer Lake and Canyon Creek Trail

Beginning at Sol Duc Falls, this trail provides a route to Hidden and Deer Lakes and to the Seven Lakes Basin.

## Hidden Lake (2800)

Containing large rainbow, this 5 acre lake may be found by hiking up Deer Lake/Canyon Creek Trail from Sol Duc Falls to a bridge crossing Canyon Creek, then contouring west approximately 0.5 miles to the lake. The outlet flows two or three hundred feet before plunging over steep cliffs to the Sol Duc River 0.5 miles below. Map and compass work required. Surrounded on all sides by forest, it is difficult to fish. There is very limited natural spawning in the inlet and outlet and neither should be fished or disturbed.

*Deer Lake. Francis Caldwell photo.*

## Deer Lakes (3525)

Hike up Canyon Creek Trail, 2.9 miles to the very popular and heavily fished Deer Lakes. The lakes total 8 acres. The smaller lake, called Fawn Pond, contains no fish, but Deer Lake holds decent size brook trout, descendants of a 1923 planting described by Webster: "85,000 eastern brook were planted in the upper Sol Duc and in Deer Lake." Historically the lake has produced rainbow as well because there is natural spawning habitat in the east inlet, which should be left unfished and pristine. The brookies run from 6–14 inches and are said to spawn in the outlet stream.

# Sol Duc: Seven Lakes Basin Lakes

It is 8 miles from the trailhead at Sol Duc Campground to the Seven Lakes Basin. Most of the lakes are iced in until late July, sometimes August.

The basin is approximately 2.5 miles long by a mile wide, very scenic and is heavily traveled. Camping restrictions are imposed. Check at Sol Duc Ranger Station for current regulations and for permits.

### Heart Lake (4700)

Reached up the Sol Duc Trail, right near its junction with the High Divide Trail, it contains no trout.

### Sol Duc Lake (3700)

This large 31 acre lake is well over 100 feet deep in the middle, contains abundant food and large numbers of shrimp. It is capable of producing large eastern brook. The average size is approximately 9 inches, with fish to 14–15 inches, making this a good angler's destination. The lake is surrounded on three sides by dense stands of trees and is difficult to fish.

### Round Lake (4300)

Small, at 3 acres and no more than 25 feet deep, this picturesque lake is not as heavily fished as some of the other Seven Lakes. The lake may have periodic spawning failures, but often has very large eastern brook to 17–18 inches.

### Lunch Lake (4350)

Lunch Lake, so–called apparently because it is the first lake to be reached when hiking to the Seven Lakes Basin and therefore a good place to eat lunch, is 7 acres and 65 feet deep. Centrally located in the basin, it is a favorite camping location, and thus is heavily fished. Although studies have found that food organisms are abundant, including fresh wa–ter shrimp, it produces eastern

*Round Lake. NPS photo.*

brook which often show evidence of stunting. There are no other species in the lake and the average size is 7–8 inches

### Lower Y Lake (4400)

Largely ignored by fishermen, Lower Y Lake, lying in a rocky glacial pocket, is approximately 6 acres and supports eastern brook. It's outlet runs into Lunch Lake. It is found by way trail from Lunch Lake. Upper Y Lake, found just upslope from Lower Y, does not contain fish.

# Long Lake (4000)

There is a very large population of eastern brook, 8 inch average size in this 50 foot deep 15 acre lake. It stretches through part of a canyon above the south wall of the Sol Duc river.

# Morganroth Lake and Noname Lake (4200)

These lakes are joined by a stream, passable in both directions to fish. They lie on the eastern edge of the Seven Lakes Basin just over a steep ridge from Long Lake. There is no trail and map and compass are necessary. Morganroth Lake is 10 acres and Noname, 7 acres. Maximum depth in Noname is 25 feet, Morganroth exceeds 60 feet. Both lakes have fresh water shrimp and are productive; they have populations of eastern brook and rainbow, brook ranging to over 15 inches, and rainbow averaging 9–11 inches.

This area was extensively rehabilitated in 1993–94; use designated sites only and do not walk on revegetated trails.

# Clear Lake (4400)

Located in a small pocket near the center of the Basin, Clear Lake does not contain fish.

# Hoh Lake (4500)

Reached either by hiking up Hoh River Trail (the long way) or by traveling beyond Seven Lakes Basin Trail approximately 2.5 miles, Hoh Lake, easily fished and very scenic, is frozen late into the season, usually to mid–July and sometimes into August. At 18 acres, it contains eastern brook.

# Haigs Lake (4675)

This 5 acre lake on the eastern edge of Seven Lakes Basin is seldom visited because there is no trail to it. It is unknown whether it contains fish.

> *"I will concede there may occasionally be a man who, having a small regard for his standing amongst the fishing fraternity, will, now and then, resort to deliberate, downright lying in the relating of an alleged fishing experience." —E. B. Webster*

# Eastern Olympics and Hood Canal

*"They went down to the river, a beautiful stream, rapids feather–
white with foam, swirling pools of the deepest green, mossy banks,
flower bedecked rocks, sunlight and shadow, vistas of ranges and
valleys between the wide–spread trees, and stepped out alongside a
large boulder in the eddying water." —E. B. Webster*

## Mount Townsend

### Townsend Creek and Sink Lake (3000)

The Mt. Townsend trail, #843, reached by a complicated road route up
FR27, begins at 2,850 feet and in 0.5 miles reaches Sink Lake. Sink Lake is
an approximately 1 acre pond and often loses its volume to become merely a
deep channel of Townsend Creek as it passes through the empty lake basin
during warm summer months. At full volume, the lake has a maximum
depth of approximately 8 feet. The outlet to Townsend Creek is on the
surface at high water, but disappears during low water to reappear 0.25 miles
below the lake. Sink Lake contains small brook trout.

Approximately 2 miles below Sink Lake, a logging road crosses Townsend
Creek. There are numerous pools in this area and downstream, holding both
cutthroat and eastern brook, the brookies about 7 inches and cutthroat averaging
6 inches with a few 8 inchers. Downstream from a falls approximately 1.5 miles
below the bridge there are predominately cutthroat with some to 8 inches.

### Silver Lakes (4920 and 5550)

Continuing along the Mt. Townsend Trail, past Sink Lake, at 4 miles,
5,650 feet, the trail forks to the Silver Lakes, reached in another 2.5 miles
and a 250 foot elevation loss. The lower lake is one acre and contains eastern
brook to 10 inches. Upper Silver Lake is two acres, an eastern brook lake
with trout to approximately 12 inches. It has a small channel which supports
spawning trout. There is a fisherman's trail all the way around the lake.

# *Quilcene*

## Quilcene River

Fishing the Quilcene River has its advantages and disadvantages. The main advantage is that it is the first river that can be fished on the east slope of the Olympic Peninsula without concern about high water.

It is small virtually everywhere, approximately a cast across, and never much more than knee–deep with an occasional beautiful hole approximately 6–10 feet deep. The best fishing is close to the road, not much of a drive off Highway 101. The fish are eager and it is easy to spend half a day catching countless small trout.

The disadvantage lies partially in the size of the trout, as a 12 incher is a mammoth fish in most of the Quilcene. Slippery rocks make for tough wading, and the river is overhung in many places with trees and bushes. There is not a lot of water to fish, but enough to keep you returning for a few trips.

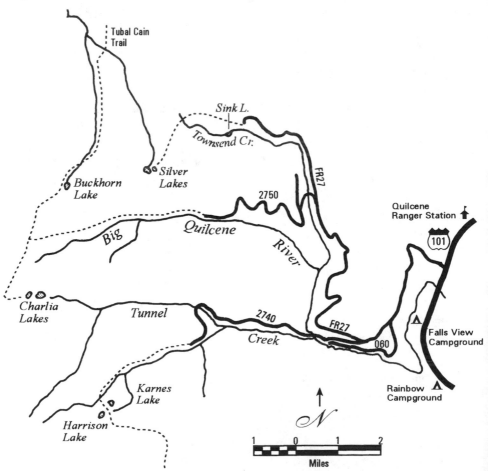

*Townsend Creek brook trout. Author photo.*

The river is reached by driving south about 1 mile from the town of Quilcene. The lower section, below the fish hatchery, runs a couple of miles down into Quilcene Bay and carries anadromous fish from the hatchery to and from salt water. During spawning season, wild anadromous fish also go up beyond the hatchery, another half–mile or more to an impassable falls, accessible from Falls View Campground.

Salmon and steelhead are readily visible in the lower river, because it is so small. There are rumored to be sea run cutthroat seasonally in this section of the river. In the fall the river gets extremely low and is almost dewatered in places; it is not a very satisfying place to fish for anadromous fish struggling to make it back to their origin, either the hatchery or the river itself.

The next section of river is found above the falls and is best accessed from the Rainbow Campground area, by hiking 0.5 miles down to the river, where it is fishable for a half–mile to the entrance of a canyon. The river is somewhat larger here than above the canyon and holds fish 4–12 inches. It is relatively easy fishing and one can catch a lot of small rainbow in this section. Most fish will be 6 inches or smaller.

Above the canyon, there is an area which is reached by following the road to the Port Townsend Dam, the point where Tunnel Creek and the big Quilcene River join. This road comes down to the river just above the upper entrance to the canyon and one can fish from here up, approximately 2–3 miles to the dam. This is the better fishing area of the two accessible non–anadromous sections of the river. Fish here might average 5 inches, but if continuous action with trout rising to a dry fly is what is most satisfying, this is the place for you. Fishing is difficult because of overhanging branches and you can expect to be hung up frequently. Fishing is prohibited in the area immediately below the dam.

Above the dam, the Quilcene is about the same size as Tunnel Creek. This is basically pothole fishing with difficult wading and tough casting. At the junction of Townsend Creek, there are some cutthroat to 12 inches. This fishing is not particularly satisfying because it is so difficult, the fish are so small, and the time spent getting one's fly out of the trees is almost equal to the time fishing.

The Washington Department of Fish and Wildlife for many years has planted rainbow in the Quilcene River, in various places below the dam. It is not clear whether these fish establish themselves and are successfully spawning and populating the river. Fishing experience suggests that few if any of these fish make it through the winter and stocking provides only a put–and–take fishery.

As with most rivers, there is a proverbial "Quilcene Canyon", which is essentially impassable, and reputed to hold 16–18 inch fish. Why it holds trout this size, and the rest of the river does not, is unknown, except that it might be possible because there are very deep holes in the canyon. Part of the canyon is visible from above the rocky cliffs leading down to it, revealing just enough to let you know that you don't want to go down into it. Apparently some fish checkers have gotten through the canyon using wet suits and have found some very large trout.

## Charlia Lakes (5400 and 5700)

Charlia Lakes, 3 and 9 acres, are most easily accessible from the Upper Big Quilcene Trail, 5.3 miles from the trailhead to Marmot Pass, then left to Boulder Shelter, and left again in another 500 feet, to the way trail to the lakes. In another mile, the ridge above the lake is attained and almost 1000 feet below, the lakes are visible. There is also a way trail to the lakes from the Upper Tunnel Creek Road using a spur off road #2740. The lower lake contains eastern brook.

## Buckhorn Lake (5100)

Difficult to find, Buckhorn is a one acre, shallow lake, which produces large numbers of small brook trout. It can be reached by either the Tubal Cain Trail, following a way trail 1.9 miles beyond Copper Creek, or at the same junction by hiking the Upper Big Quilcene Trail to Marmot Pass, turning right, and traveling to that junction, approximately 7 miles. This is the more scenic of the two routes.

## Harrison Lake (4750)

The 3.7 mile trail to Harrison Lake begins at 2600 feet at the end of road #2740, also called the Tunnel Creek Road. This lake can also be reached from the Dosewallips Road, but the average grade is 40% in the first 3 miles and only lunatics try to get there from this side. Harrison Lake is 0.7 of an acre and approximately 5 feet deep in most places, with a maximum depth of 8–10 feet. Eastern brook have been reproducing in this lake naturally for years and it is full of fish no larger than 8-9 inches.

## Karnes Lake (4600)

Located 0.5 miles north from Harrison Lake, Karnes produces small eastern brook. Consult your map.

# *Dosewallips*

## Dosewallips River

The Dosewallips is generally high early in the season and off–color because of glacial melt from aptly named Silt Creek, which flows into the mainstem of the Dosewallips several miles above its junction with the West Fork, inside the Park boundary. Downstream from this point, the river is colored by glacial melt at least until early July, and often into August.

The lower river, from Hood Canal to an impassable falls 13.7 miles up Dosewallips Road, becomes fishable for trout after its water level drops. The lower river is essentially an anadromous fish river and fishing for steelhead, salmon and sea–run cutthroat is found in the lower Dosewallips. There are trout here, but not sufficient numbers to recommend fishing for them lower than about 6–7 miles up the road. Much of the lower road is in private ownership, but public access can be had in numerous places up to the falls.

*Dosewallips River. NPS photo.*

Despite its opacity, the Dosewallips is fishable once its water level drops. Extreme care should be exercised when wading. Nymph fishing is most successful, but when the river's clarity improves it is readily fishable with dry flies.

Probably due to competition with anadromous fish, there seem to be a lot less trout in the section of river below the falls. Below the falls, trout are much less heavily spotted and colored and probably fish caught are mostly immature steelhead, rather than rainbow. It is obvious that these fish are of a different strain than the ones above the falls. Trout can be caught in the lower river but it is hard work and

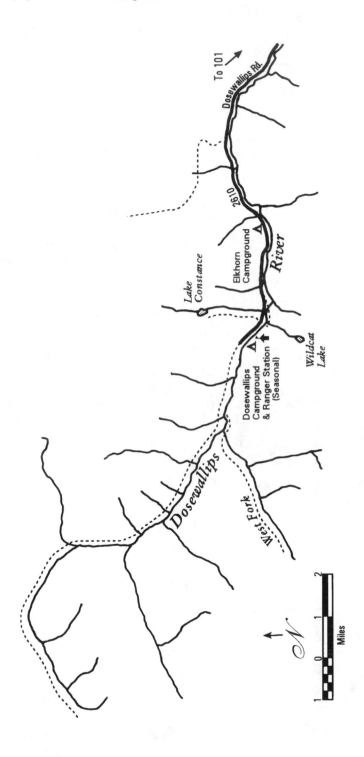

they seem to be smaller. Wading is more difficult and the river is larger, adding to the problems.

Above the falls, there is a good mile of fishable water accessible from the road until its end is reached, where the Dosewallips Trail begins, leading far upriver to the West Fork and Anderson Pass, as well as up the mainstem to Hayden Pass. The river may be fished by slogging upstream from the parking lot or by dropping down to the river along the trail. This water is enjoyable to fish, has plenty of good holding water, and some deep holes. There are a good number of rainbow trout in each likely place. The average fish is about 8 inches, but there are some to 11–12 inches. The trout are, in most instances, fat, heavily spotted and some have deep red stripes. There are eastern brook in the headwater area and a population of Yellowstone cutthroat in the canyon area near Camp Marion, 8.3 miles from the trailhead.

The clear water of the West Fork offers good fishing for rainbow along its length, much of which is accessible from the trail to Anderson Pass. The mainstem is seasonally glacially colored above the West Fork to its juncture with Silt Creek, but is clear above this point and provides good fishing for small trout.

## Lake Constance (1650)

The Lake Constance Trail is only 2 miles long but gains a very steep 3,250 feet from the trailhead, which begins at Constance Creek, within 0.5 miles of the Park entrance on the Dosewallips Road. Surprisingly, despite this very strenuous hike, the lake tends to be crowded. Camping is by quota system only and lake water is sometimes polluted. Check with the Hood Canal Ranger Station for the latest regulations.

Constance is a very deep lake, surrounded on three sides by high walls and talus slopes, its clear blue water mirroring the surrounding woods and peaks. It has a large population of stunted eastern brook, average 8 inches, some to 10 inches and slightly larger. Fish often school up in deeper water, particularly on sunny days and can be difficult to catch.

The difficulty of this hike combined with the size and condition of the fish deters most anglers from visiting Constance.

## Wildcat Lake (4150)

Wildcat Lake is an approximately 5 acre lake at the head of Tumbling Creek, which flows into the Dosewallips River about 0.3 miles upriver from the mouth of Constance Creek. Fanatics have claimed it is possible to bushwhack up Tumbling Creek approximately 1–2 miles to Wildcat Lake. Saner fishermen, always armed with map and compass, get to this lake by hiking up Muscott Basin Trail, an unmaintained trail, extremely difficult to follow, that starts from the old Dosewallips Trail, which is reached by crossing the river (difficult to do and dangerous when the river is high) at the upper jump–off, at a packer's station just above Dosewallips Falls. This trail continues parallel to, but above, the river. In about a mile a primitive trail begins climbing up from the Dosewallips, leading eventually to what was long ago the site of Muscott Cabin, an old prospector cabin, long maintained by the Forest Service, then abandoned. The trail follows Muscott Creek and eventually crosses the creek at approximately 2 miles. Map work and serious cross–country effort bring the hiker to Muscott Basin. By hiking to the next basin to the east, one can find Wildcat Lake at the head of Tumbling Creek. Eastern brook inhabit the lake.

# *Jupiter Ridge*

### Jupiter Lakes (3800)

The trailhead to the Jupiter Lakes is located at the end of Mt. Jupiter Road #2620, which begins on Highway 101, opposite Black Point, 0.9 miles north of Duckabush River Road and 3 miles south of Dosewallips River Road. The road forks at 3.7 miles. Turn left on road #2620–011 to the trailhead, which begins 6.4 miles from Highway 101.

This is a strenuous, but rewarding hike, in which a climb to the summit

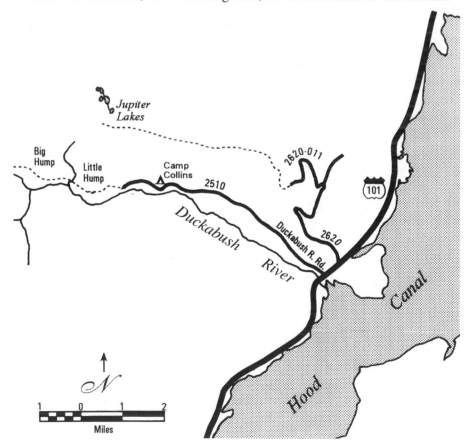

of Mt. Jupiter can be combined with camping at the Jupiter Lakes, all accomplished by hiking slightly over 7 miles from the trailhead. However, these 7 miles, after the first 1 mile climb, have a great deal of downhill hiking which must be followed by considerable uphill hiking, then more downhill and alas, continued uphill hiking. It is essential to bring water on this hike. Approximately 0.5 miles from the summit there is a chute which leads down to Jupiter Lakes. By working down among boulders and rock slides 600 feet, the three Jupiter Lakes are found. Two other seldom visited Jupiter Lakes are accessible by continuing past Mt. Jupiter to its northwest side. Map and compass are required.

The highest of the lakes, 4,000 feet, has 3 surface acres. Its maximum depth is 20 feet. The second lake is 1.5 acres and lies at an elevation of 3,800 feet, approximately 15 feet deep. The third, at 3,850 feet, 6 acres, is the largest of the Jupiter Lakes, approximately 50 feet deep near its center.

In the original stocking of these lakes, rainbow and cutthroat were planted in the highest lake, and only rainbow in the second and third lakes reached by hiking down from Mt. Jupiter. In a survey taken in 1972 after the stocking, the highest lake was found to have large rainbow, averaging 14 inches, cutthroat averaging 11; the largest lake, rainbow averaging 12 inches; the third lake, rainbow averaging approximately 11 inches. It was recommended in 1973 that the Jupiter Lakes be planted every 4 years and it appears the stocking policy is continuing as recommended.

It is unknown whether the two lakes on the other side of the ridge contain trout. They are extremely difficult to find, but may well be worth trying.

# Duckabush

### Duckabush River

The Duckabush River Road extends approximately 6.5 miles from Highway 101 to its end, where the trail to the upper river begins. Trout in the lower Duckabush must compete with salmon and steelhead. Nevertheless, it appears that because of less competition resulting from diminution of anadromous runs, trout are doing better in the lower Duckabush than in most lower Olympic rivers.

The first real access to the lower river is at Ranger Hole. A sign on the road leads to a 0.5 mile walk to very deep, beautiful holes popular with steelhead fishermen. There are trout and steelhead smolt in this area, in the 8–10 inch range. Above Ranger Hole, the next good access is just before the Gauging Station, where a cable car crosses the river. Fishing continues much the same, but the trout are slightly larger. The river is about a cast across and there are deep holes in some sections here, but it is extremely difficult to get fish to rise to a fly from the bottom of these pools.

*Duckabush River at Ten-mile shelter. NPS photo.*

Access is consistent along the Duckabush above the Gauging Station, to a bridge crossing a mile above Camp Collins Campground. At the bridge there is good access down to the river. With some effort, one can continue on up the river and eventually come out at the point where the Duckabush comes close enough to the upper river trail, after it has crossed the Little Hump, to then turn around and hike back out the trail if so inclined. This is pretty much an all–day proposition, and the going is not particularly easy. However, at low water in August and September this can be done without a great deal of difficulty, fishing a lot of water.

The upper Duckabush provides many miles of pleasant and scenic hike–in fishing. It is approximately 2 miles from the Duckabush trailhead to just over the Little Hump, an easy 45 minute walk to the river. The trail flattens, and the river is approximately a hundred yards away to the left. There are numerous side trails and hunting camps located in this area which will allow you to get over to the river with some minor thrashing through the woods. There is a good stretch of river from here up to the beginning of the Big Hump, approximately half a mile. You can also go downstream from here, at low water, and fish all the way out to below the Little Hump, intersecting with the road, slightly above Camp Collins where the bridge crosses the river.

The upper river has some holes that are waist–deep and the fish are slightly more reluctant to rise from deep down in these holes. Beyond the reach of anadromous fish, this is entirely trout water, with rainbow averaging from 6-10 inches. A 12 incher is a lunker.

Continuing on the trail after reaching the river past the Little Hump, hikers grind up the 89 switchbacks to the Big Hump and down to the river again, an elevation gain of 1000 feet in a mile, followed by a corresponding descent to the river. Above the Big Hump, fishing is reputed to be "better," as there are more trout, though few of any real size.

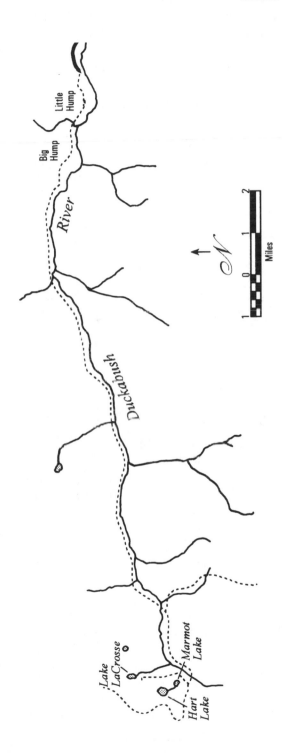

Fish caught in the Duckabush are usually fat and healthy and there seem to be more insect hatches than are found in some of the other east side rivers.

There are excellent camping spots above the Little Hump and beyond the Big Hump.

## Marmot Lakes (4350), Hart Lake (4900) and La Crosse Lake (4750)

It takes a journey to the end of the Duckabush River Trail to fish and explore the Marmot Lakes, Hart Lake, and Lake La Crosse. This hike can be continued on through O'Neal Pass and out through either the Quinault or the Dosewallips. It is a long hike requiring several nights. The lakes are generally frozen until mid–July and sometimes even into August. Marmot Lakes, lying in a shallow depression below the east summit of O'Neal Pass, are the first reached, at approximately 21 miles in on the Duckabush Trail. Hart Lake is 0.5 miles above the Marmot Lakes in a cirque, and Lake La Crosse, in a spectacular setting, 1.5 miles further along the main trail.

Hart is l6 acres, La Crosse approximately 3 acres and Marmot Lake is approximately 4 acres. Of the three, only Hart Lake is known to contain trout.

# Hamma Hamma

## Hamma Hamma River

The Hamma Hamma River, from its mouth at Highway 101 to a large falls 3–4 miles upriver, is anadromous fish territory. There are a few resident rainbow, some steelhead, and runs of chinook, coho, pink and chum salmon which use the river, but this is not really a trout fishing area. Access to the lower river is all through private land, but the family which lives just above the 101 bridge has been known to give permission to fish in this section of river during steelhead season for a modest fee. The lower river and its surroundings are pristine, resembling a national park in the abundance of wildlife and the unspoiled nature of the environment. There has been some logging and there is farming but very little has been changed in this lower valley.

The upper Hamma Hamma is reached by two roads. The Hamma Hamma Road is paved and is a nice road, but access to the river is better on the gravel Jorstad Creek Road. Most trout fishing on the upper Hamma Hamma occurs between the access points along the Jorstad Creek and the Hamma Hamma roads up to the junction of Lena Creek with the Hamma Hamma.

Above this junction, the Hamma Hamma is smaller, brushier, more difficult to fish and access is often through dense woods. Surprisingly, well

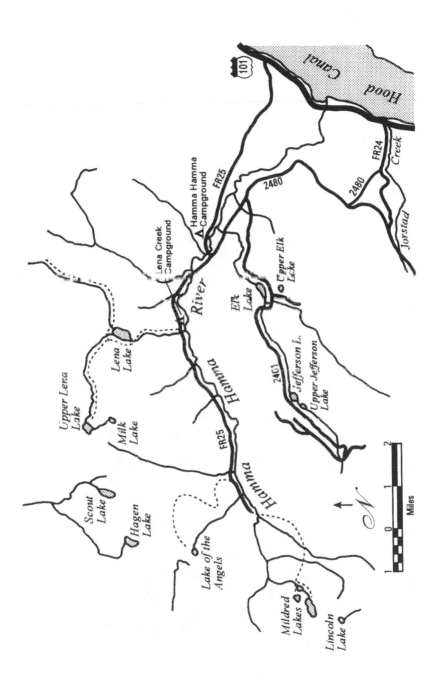

above the Lena Creek junction, there are larger average fish, conceivably because there has been no planting for years, and natural selection has reduced the numbers somewhat. However, fishing is extremely difficult because of brush, overhanging trees, slippery rocks, and lack of any large holes. It's hard work, you're likely to fall in, and anglers feel beaten up after rock–hopping and bashing through the trees. Nevertheless, it is isolated, pristine, few anglers fish there, and the trout will rise to a fly.

Below the junction of Lena Creek and downstream to the falls, the river is full of rainbow trout. The Washington Department of Fish and Wildlife stocks rainbow, 8–10 inchers, in this section annually in three, staggered plantings This stocking follows a very old tradition in Washington State where trout were pumped into the river just prior to major camping weekends, so that campers would have fish to catch. With the increasing popularity of fly fishing, there is some doubt whether these fish are being caught at the rate they were when most people fished with bait.

There is the occasional 12 inch rainbow in this section, but they are few and far between. Generally, one catches 5–8 inch rainbow. These little trout are fun, because they rise willingly to a dry fly. A semi–decent drift through pocket water or through the upper or lower end of a hole, will usually yield lots of rising fish. Once in awhile, an 11–12 inch behemoth will lose its senses and smash the fly, causing near cardiac arrest in older fishermen.

An occasional bigger fish can be dredged up from the bottom throughout the season. This is particularly true in late summer and in early September, when larger fish, many of which are the current year's plants, will move into faster water and hunger will drive them to take a dry fly.

Very few planted trout, if any, will hold over to the next year. If there are any, they do not seem to grow appreciably in the meantime.

*Hamma Hamma River. Author photo.*

The Hamma Hamma is probably the most beautiful of all the eastside rivers. The color of the water is extraordinary, very clear, with many deep blue pools. It is bordered by more deciduous trees than most mountain rivers and there are lots of branches overhanging, heavily covered with moss. It is frequented by deer and elk and sightings are not too unusual in the evenings in sections which are not often fished.

The Hamma Hamma may have the most abundant trout population of the east side rivers but unfortunately it also has the most substantial number of small fish. It is not uncommon to catch what appear to be fully mature, beautifully marked and dark 5 7 inch fish. While it seems that larger trout could live in this river, very few do and the little fish that are here are well-adapted to their environment. Neither starving nor in bad shape, most of them are very healthy and are appropriately proportioned to their length.

## Lower Lena Lake (1900)

The approximately 3 mile trail to Lower Lena Lake is one of the most heavily used trails in the State of Washington. The trailhead is 7.7 miles from Highway 101, easily found because of the large number of cars parked on the road. The lake is extremely deep, 155 feet, and at 55 acres it is the largest and deepest lake lying totally within Olympic National Forest. It will drop as much as 18 feet each year during the course of the summer. The lake is difficult to fish from shore and a floating device of some kind is advised.

Extensive studies of Lena have found aquatic insects to be very abundant both in the lake and its major tributary, Lena Creek. Mayfly, caddis, midge larvae, and, of course, mosquito larvae, along with aquatic beetles, are numerous in the littoral zone. Stone fly nymphs are found in Lena Creek, as are mayfly nymphs and caddis larvae.

Lower Lena Lake contains rainbow, eastern brook and cutthroat. The average size rainbow is approximately 10 inches, brook trout, about 8 inches.

The lake historically has been heavily planted, most often with cutthroat. Trout spawn in Lena Creek above the lake into July, and because of severe angler pressure on the spawning population in the creek, the spawning grounds have been closed to fishing. The Forest Service estimates that Lower Lena receives more fishing pressure every summer than any other high lake in Olympic National Forest and more than most lowland lakes on the Olympic Peninsula.

## Upper Lena Lake (4450)

The trail from Lower Lena to Upper Lena is 4 miles, the last one of which is discouragingly steep, but not enough to deter substantial numbers of campers and anglers. The lake is 26 acres and has several inlet streams, including one which feeds it from Milk Lake, as well as an outlet stream. There is a healthy population of self-sustaining rainbow.

*Upper Lena Lake. NPS photo.*

Due to heavy use, the area around the lake has been extensively rehabilitated. Camp only in designated areas and do not use closed and revegetated social trails.

## Milk Lake (4750)

Milk Lake is located approximately 0.5 miles above Upper Lena Lake and can be easily found by following the creek between Milk Lake and Upper Lena Lake south, a 300 feet elevation gain. There is no information on the status of fish in the lake.

## Scout Lake (4250)

A 3 mile unmaintained way trail to Scout begins on the west shore of Upper Lena Lake, and ends in a descent of nearly seven hundred feet in the last 0.5 miles. The verticality and heavy vegetation of its surroundings make this 15 acre lake difficult to fish. It contains naturally spawning rainbow, growing to substantial size, 12–17 inches. No camping is permitted at Scout Lake.

## Stone Ponds (4600)

A 1.2 mile way trail to the ponds begins at the south end of Scout Lake, 0.4 miles back on the trail toward Upper Lena Lake and heads south towards Mt. Stone. The larger of the two lakes, 3 acres, is said to contain trout, species unknown.

## Hagen Lakes (4700)

The Hagen Lakes, named for a fisheries biologist who long ago studied the lakes of the Olympics, are reached by cross–country hiking from Scout Lake, or from the First Divide using the Mt. Hopper way trail. Map and compass work are required.

For a shorter and much more direct route, a brutal, but rewarding hike, is recommended. The Putvin Trail begins approximately 12.2 miles from Highway 101 on the Hamma Hamma Road. At 3 miles, a much needed rest can be taken at Lake of the Angels. While not historically containing trout, the lake has been planted from time to time by private individuals or clubs and is worth checking to see if it contains trout. The trail weaves cross–country through the saddle between Mt. Skokomish and Mt. Stone and steeply down to Hagen Lakes, another approximately 1.5–2 miles. The largest lake is 23 acres and contains naturally reproducing rainbow. Some very large fish, up to 20 inches, have been caught in this lake. At least one of the other lakes also contains rainbow with two smaller ones not believed to hold any fish. There are 5 lakes in all in this basin.

## Mildred Lakes (3850)

The 4.9 mile trail to the Mildred Lakes begins at the end of the Hamma Hamma Road, approximately 13 miles from Highway 101. The Mildred Lakes have become a popular fishing destination and justifiably so.

The first lake one reaches, curiously designated by the Forest Service as Mildred Lake #2, is 6.5 acres. The largest lake is designated #1, 40 acres and the third lake, #3, 12 acres. Lake #3 has historically been stocked with cutthroat and has produced some very large fish. It contains substantial quantities of freshwater shrimp, *gammarus.*

Mildred #1 & #2 both have populations of rainbow trout and there are abundant 15 inch and larger rainbow in Mildred #1. Fish in Mildred #2 tend to be smaller and historically Mildred #3 has produced the largest, which are all cutthroat. Mildred #1 and #2 are not stocked with any regularity because there is natural reproduction occurring. Care should be taken not to disturb the stream between the two lakes, and the outlet stream, which provide the primary spawning habitat. A raft or float tube is strongly recommended for Mildred #1 as trolling produces significantly more fish in this very fine fishing lake than does shore casting.

*Hagen Lake.*
*NPS photo.*

# Lincoln Lakes (4600)

The largest Lincoln Lake, designated #1, lies at the head of Slate Creek, approximately 1 mile from the southwest shore of Mildred Lake #1. It contains trout. While fishermen have found their way up to Lincoln Lakes from this direction, access is extremely difficult and requires map, compass and route–finding skills. A more likely route is north and west from Wagonwheel Lake, following the ridge forming the park–forest boundary. Exercise extreme caution using either route.

# Elk Lake (1051)

Elk Lake is reached by taking the Jorstad Creek Road from Highway 101, approximately 1 mile south of Eldon, then turning up road #2401 to Elk Lake, or by taking the Hamma Hamma Road to the bridge across the Hamma Hamma River and then down the Jorstad Creek Road to the same junction with road #2401.

The surface area of Elk Lake varies from 6–10 acres, depending upon snow pack, rainfall and time of year. This pleasant lake was once considerably larger, but due to siltation from logging, much of it has filled in. It will probably continue to do so until at some point there may not be any more Elk Lake.

In the meantime, though, fishing is surprisingly good. While most of the lake is quite shallow, it reaches 15–20 feet deep in a couple of spots. Trout tend to be concentrated in the deep pockets and the inlet channels. At times there have been cutthroat and rainbow planted in this lake, and there is limited spawning by both in the inlet streams. The lake contains mostly eastern brook, some of which reach good size, and to the delight of dry fly anglers, there is a lot of surface feeding.

There is an approximately 1 mile trail circling Elk Lake providing access to most of the lake, including the inlets.

# Upper Elk Lake (1200)

Just beyond Elk Lake, the road forks and the left fork, within less than half a mile, passes Upper Elk Lake on its left. Upper Elk Lake is a classic mountain lake of 3 acres, 60 feet deep, has a reproducing population of small brookies and is periodically stocked with cutthroat. A study of this lake, the results of which may have general application to high lake fishing technique, found that the brook trout were generally close to bottom around the littoral zone and the cutthroat were in the top 20 feet of the water, spread across the lake.

# Lower and Upper Jefferson Lakes (1800)

Continuing up road #2401 from Elk Lake, the road crosses and then follows Jefferson Creek, which contains trout, but is too small to really be worth fishing. Eventually, the road passes Lower Jefferson Lake on the left. The lake is 10 acres and is very deep. There is a nice spawning stream

*Upper Jefferson Lake. Author photo.*

flowing into it from Upper Jefferson Lake and it contains trout until they move out of it in low water, or until it is fished out. This lake will drop as much as 25–30 feet during a warm summer.

Upper Jefferson Lake was formed by a slide which separated it from Lower Jefferson Lake. At its largest, it covers 3 surface acres, but will drop about 3 feet during summer. Much like lower Elk Lake, it is in danger of disappearing due to siltation from logging.

Rainbow to 12 inches, eastern brook to 15 inches and cutthroat up to 9 inches are caught in the lakes. The rainbow and cutthroat are natural spawners and the stream connecting the two lakes should not be fished or disturbed in any way. This is the sole habitat which allows the rainbow and cutthroat to spawn, which in high mountain lakes for trout other than eastern brook is relatively rare because so few have inlet or outlet streams with sufficient spawning habitat.

Historically, these lakes provided some very large trout for local fishermen. They are fished rather heavily, but still maintain plentiful populations of trout and a good fly fishing experience.

## Goober Pond (3200)

Continuing up road #2401, past Upper Jefferson Lake, the road ends at a T. The right fork, in approximately 1.5 miles, crosses a creek and above this creek is located Goober Pond. Goober Pond is a small, round, approximately 0.75 acre lake which historically has contained both rainbow and eastern brook as it has been periodically planted with both species. It is a healthy, productive pond.

## Pershing Lake (5000)

Approximately 1.5 miles northwest of Goober Pond lies Pershing Lake. This is a difficult cross–country climb requiring map and compass. In 1990 the State of Washington planted golden trout in this lake.

# Lake Cushman

## Price's Lake

Price's Lake is an excellent fly fishing lowland lake reached by driving up Lake Cushman road 7 miles from Highway 101, then east approximately 1.5 miles to the lake. After turning right off Lake Cushman Road, just south of the turnoff to Lake Cushman State Park, the road forks in approximately a mile. The left fork leads to a 0.1 mile trail to the right to Price's Lake. The right fork leads to a semi–abandoned road and 0.4 miles to the southwest part of Price's Lake.

This lake gets more and more difficult to locate as the roads degenerate. Its outlet drains into Lilliwaup Creek and there are numerous beaver ponds in this area for dedicated sloggers and bushwhackers.

There was a resort on Price's Lake for many years which rented boats which were serviceable only after a lot of bailing and payment of $3. About the time the last boat was no longer bailable, the remnants of the resort burned to the ground. The proprietors, when asked what kind of fly to use, invariably replied, "Pink Lady." This fly was sold at the resort, along with worms and very little else.

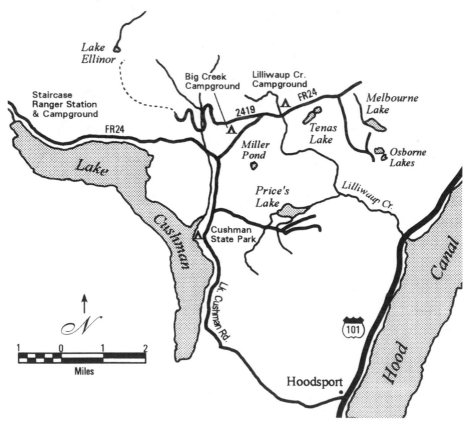

The lake was once managed as a wild eastern brook lake and a few brookies grew to large size, but the lake lost its appeal to many. It is now regularly planted with cutthroat, rainbow and eastern brook. Trout grow to 18–20 inches in its fertile waters. Special regulations have long applied to Price's Lake.

## Lilliwaup Swamp

There are numerous beaver ponds in the area near Price's Lake. There are also some sizable lakes, many of which are reachable only by walking, as roads dead–end or are washed out.

Miller Pond is reached by continuing on the left fork of the road to Price's Lake, past another left, to a junction with a road leading to the right. Take a left, continue on, take a right at the next junction, and a left at the final junction to the road end. Miller Pond is due north at this point.

By driving north on the Lake Cushman Road past the Price's Lake turnoff, to the "T" at the end of the road, then turning right onto FR24, in approximately 2.5 miles to the right, not visible, however, is Tenas Lake. At approximately 3 miles on FR24 there is an old logging road which leads to the Osborne Lakes, Melbourne Lake and several other small ponds. All of these lakes and ponds contain trout. Tenas Lake contains eastern brook and rainbow. Melbourne is stocked with rainbow and cutthroat, and Miller Pond has cutthroat. Osborne Lake is regularly planted with rainbow.

Considerable exploration is required to find each of these lakes, but all contain fish and are worth the effort. A boat or a float tube is almost a necessity as back–casting from shore is nearly impossible in these brushy, swampy lakes and ponds.

Osborne, Tenas and Melbourne are heavily fished on opening day. It's better to try them late in the season.

## Lake Cushman

This enormous reservoir created by damming (some say damning) the North Fork Skokomish River can provide some excellent fishing, primarily at its inlet, at various times of the season. The former channel of the Skokomish River exists underneath all that water at the lake's north end and trout like to hang out in the area of this channel. Large rainbow, cutthroat, kokanee, and even chinook salmon have been caught here. Fall is generally the best time to fish this area, as the chinook, kokanee and Dolly Varden all run into the North Fork to spawn. They are generally followed by rainbow and cutthroat. Knowledgeable anglers have had outstanding fishing here at times.

## Lake Ellinor (4000)

Lake Ellinor is reached from Trail #812, which climbs to the peak of Mt. Ellinor. The 6 acre lake lies approximately 1 mile north in the drainage of Jefferson Creek, directly behind and below Mt. Ellinor.

The Mt. Ellinor trail is reached by turning right onto road #2419 at the 7.2 mile mark of FR 24. There are two trailheads. The upper trailhead at the end of road #2419–014 cuts about 1.5 miles off the trip. From there it is approximately a mile and almost 2000 vertical feet to the point where one can contour around Mt. Ellinor to the headwaters of Jefferson Creek and then on down a steep mile, to the lake.

Lake Ellinor may also be reached by bushwhacking up Jefferson Creek from the point where the road crosses Jefferson Creek above Upper Jefferson Lake (see Hamma Hamma). Take the road above Upper Jefferson to its end at a "T," turn right, crossing Jefferson Creek in approximately 0.25 miles. By staying above the creek on the left and following the contours of the ridge, Ellinor can be reached in approximately 2 miles. This is not a particularly difficult bushwhack. Along the way you may pass the remnants of a small airplane which crashed there long ago.

The lake is approximately 6 to15 feet deep, contains rainbow and it is planted once approximately every 5 years, because there is no natural spawning habitat.

# North Fork Skokomish

## North Fork Skokomish River

The Skokomish River, above Lake Cushman, called the North Fork, is almost entirely located in Olympic National Park. The Park Service has decreed it a catch–and–release fishery and it is a fine place to fly fish. Updated special regulation information is available through the Hood Canal Ranger Station.

The exquisite North Fork waters are so clear that you can see every stone on the bottom. The river is unaffected by glacial melt and tends to diminish in volume early, so it is often fishable in June.

From the Staircase Ranger Station, one can begin fishing immediately or walk up Staircase Trail approximately a mile to the Staircase Bridge and Staircase Rapids. The river below Staircase Rapids contains some very large Dolly Varden. Lake Cushman chinook salmon, up to 20 plus pounds, descendants of a formerly anadromous population but resident since the days of the Cushman Dam, use the river for spawning. There are kokanee from the lake, and cutthroat and rainbow travel up into the river to spawn. Fall is a great time to watch a variety of spawning fish in the river above Lake Cushman, but not a good time to fish the North Fork below Staircase Rapids because the Park Service closes this section of the river to fishing to protect the spawning runs. There are also plenty of resident trout in this section of the river, although few grow to much bigger than 12 inches.

Above Staircase Rapids the river flattens out a bit, wading is easier, and it is definitely worth the walk. There are a fair number of fish to 14 inches and they fight extremely well. Rainbow predominate in this section of the

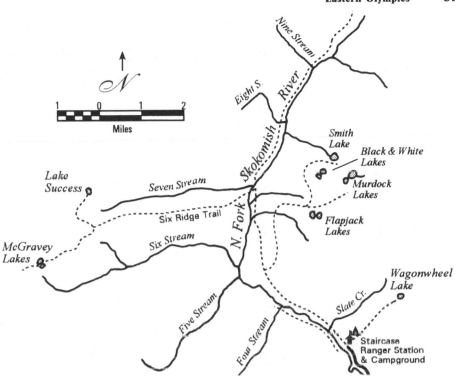

river and there are some Dolly Varden as well as cutthroat, most of the
cutthroat apparently having moved into the river from Lake Cushman to
spawn in April and May before working back down to the lake through the
summer. Whitefish also populate this area.

Mayfly patterns, Adams and its cousins and the ever reliable Elk Hair
Caddis will work best for you. This is not easy fishing because drag is hard
to avoid, and a fish hooked in a hole in this crystal water will spook the
entire hole; then you might as well move on or take a short nap.

Trails continue up the North Fork above Staircase Rapids for several
miles, and it is fishable most of the way. A few eastern brook reside in the
higher reaches along with the other species common in the North Fork.

Many of the larger tributary streams contain fish populations. Four, Five,
Six, Seven, Eight and Nine Streams all have rainbow, as do Slate, Madeline,
Donohue and Hammer Creeks. Do not expect to encounter large trout in
these streams however.

Fishing the North Fork is considerably more rewarding than most of the
other streams on the east side, probably due to the Park Service's catch–
and–release policy. Possibly the North Fork has a richer food base, but it
doesn't have that appearance. It may also be more productive because it is
necessary to hike a distance to fish, and its resident trout do not have to
compete with planted hatchery trout.

This is a fragile fishery, especially above Staircase Rapids, and there is

some question about whether
the fish population can handle
the possible mortality from
heavy fishing, even though it
is catch–and–release. Tread
lightly and release fish carefully, for this is a rare fishing
experience in Western Washington.

## Snow Lake (3700)

Snow Lake is the source of
Four Stream, which flows into
the North Fork Skokomish a
little more than 2 miles up the
North Fork Skokomish Trail
from the trailhead. This was the
site of the 1890 O'Neal
Expedition's Camp Number 4.
Although there are remnants of
an old trail up Four Stream, it
is not maintained and not recommended as an access route.
The lake is reached via cross–

*North Fork Skokomish River. NPS photo.*

country route from a spur of road #2451. Map work is required to find the
lake. Check with the Hood Canal Ranger Station in Hoodsport.

The lake is 6 acres and very deep in the middle. There is no natural
reproduction and it depends upon stocking for its fish population. Check
with the State of Washington for information regarding plants. It has been
known to provide excellent fishing at times.

## Wagonwheel Lake (4150)

This 3 acre lake has a maximum depth of 45 feet. It is located at the end
of a trail starting from the parking lot behind Staircase Ranger Station,
which gains a steep 3000 feet in 2.9 miles. This small lake is very rich and
can produce large fish. It was included within the Park during the most
recent boundary changes and the only fish present are a remnant from
stocking which occurred prior to the boundary changes.

## Flapjack Lakes (3900)

Flapjack Lakes are reached by hiking 3.7 miles up the North Fork
Skokomish Trail, then another 5.6 miles, an elevation gain of 3500 feet.
Upper Flapjack is 10 acres, maximum depth 18 feet. Lower Flapjack is 6
acres with a depth of approximately 30 feet. Connected by a stream, both
lakes are very productive and contain fresh water shrimp.

The lakes are on camping quota restrictions and a permit is required to stay overnight. Check with the Hood Canal Ranger Station for current information. Both have naturally reproducing rainbow to 11 inches, eastern brook to 14 inches and although heavily fished, provide very good fishing for healthy populations of both species.

## Smith Lake (3900)

Smith Lake is located by leaving the Flapjack Lake trail at mile 3.6, turning at Donahue Creek. Pass an abandoned mine and the path to Black & White Lakes on your way to Smith Lake, 2.1 miles. The lake lies in a small deep basin at the head of Hammer Creek, a very steep drop of several hundred feet to its shore. It is 11 acres and contains eastern brook.

## Black & White Lakes (4200)

It is said that an early group of elk hunters carved the name of their favorite whiskey into a tree at their nearby camp, thus the name of the lakes. More likely it is named for the Black & White Mine which was operated into the 1940's. While one can reach the Black & White Lakes by hiking 2 miles from a trail beginning at mile 5.5 of the North Fork Skokomish Trail, opposite Big Log Camp, it is much easier to reach them by turning left off the Flapjack Lakes Trail and hiking 1.2 miles to the lakes. (See Smith Lake). There are three Black & White Lakes only one of which is large enough to hold fish, but it is reported to be devoid of trout.

## Murdock Lakes (4000)

Cross country hiking from Gladys Divide above Flapjack Lakes will take fishermen to the two Murdock Lakes. It is unknown whether trout exist in these lakes, but by appearances they may be capable of holding a self-sustaining population of trout.

## McGravey Lakes (4000)

8.5 miles up Six Ridge Trail, which in turn begins 5.9 miles up the North Fork Skokomish Trail, lie the McGravey Lakes, approximately 1 acre each, believed to have no trout. Continuing beyond McGravey Lakes another approximately 2 miles, there is an unnamed lake at 4000 feet. It is also unknown whether trout exist in this lake.

Both lakes may also be reached by traveling up the South Fork Skokomish Trail, 6.9 miles to Sundown Pass, then 3 more miles by trail.

## Lake Success (4200)

Lake Success, is reached by turning right off Six Ridge Trail onto Mt. Olson Trail. It is unknown whether there are trout in this lake.

*"Here in the Olympics, one will not go too far wrong if his kit be limited to a piece of line and two or three brown hackles wound around the crown of his old hat."* —*E. B. Webster*

# Southern Olympics

*"It was a monster trout, a Rainbow, a silvery Rainbow, its sides gleaming with the first rosy flush of dawn—if you were ever up early enough of a summer's morning you will know what I mean."*
*—E. B. Webster*

## South Fork Skokomish

### South Fork Skokomish River

The South Fork Skokomish River is reached by driving up Forest Service Road 23, also known as the Skokomish Valley Road, from Highway 101. Most visitors to the South Fork stop and begin fishing at Brown Creek Campground, 17 miles from 101. Fishing below the campground is not rewarding, primarily because of intense pressure from numerous campsites and easy access. The valley here is also filled with gravel washes, the river only a narrow channel in the middle. For a distance downstream, the river runs through this flat area with very few pools and riffles.

Above Brown Creek Campground, the Lower South Fork Trail begins. Instead of taking the trail at its beginning some anglers fish up through a canyon, scenic but fished very hard, which begins near the trailhead and continues, approximately 1 mile to the next valley area. There the river again broadens and runs through considerable washed out gravel and then up into a narrower, treed valley as one continues up the South Fork.

Above the canyon, the river holds more fish, to 12 inches and better and there is a chance from here upriver to hook larger trout. There are rumors of 18–19 inch rainbows being caught at logjam areas and since there is so much knocked down timber, there are indeed numerous logjams in the area above the canyon where fish tend to congregate in slower water and cover. There are a few summer run steelhead which come up this far and perhaps these are the 18-19 inch "rainbow" which are reported.

To get to the area above the canyon, continue up the road from the campground, and in approximately a mile there is a road off to the left which leads to the Lower South Fork Skokomish Trail and down to the river, approximately 1 mile. You can also begin this trail just above Brown Creek, but only if you're interested in starting the day with two or three hundred feet of upward aerobic exercise which takes you far above the river. Either way you get there, after you reach the river, it is easy to walk along the washed–out gravel and fish as far upriver as desired.

The lower trail follows the river for almost 9 miles, but roads also continue paralleling the trail, providing access on both sides of the river for much of these 9 miles. The road on the north side only follows the river about half as far and then dead–ends, but it provides closer access. The road on the south side, road #2319, continues to its end just above Camp Harps where the Upper South Fork Skokomish Trail begins.

In approximately 1 mile the Upper South Fork Skokomish Trail crosses Rule Creek. The river above Rule Creek passes through an area known as "the meadows," where it is approximately 10 feet wide and 3 feet deep. This area has been studied and found to contain a native population of non–migratory cutthroat. The cutthroat spawn in the four tributaries to the main stream. The trout, though not large, are numerous and do reach 12+ inches and a few reach 15 inches. This area is very fragile and deserves extreme care by fishermen. In the future, catch–and release restrictions would be appropriate.

For some distance below Rule Creek, few anadromous fish penetrate the South Fork. The South Fork from this point on down to LeBar Creek provides good fishing for resident rainbow, some cutthroat and a few Dolly Varden.

In the winter of 1995, severe flooding washed out the road to the Upper South Fork Trail and washed out the road above Camp Brown at approximately 4.5 miles. Thus, access to the South Fork was severely reduced, at least until the washouts are repaired.

*Southern Olympic Mountain lake brook trout. Author photo.*

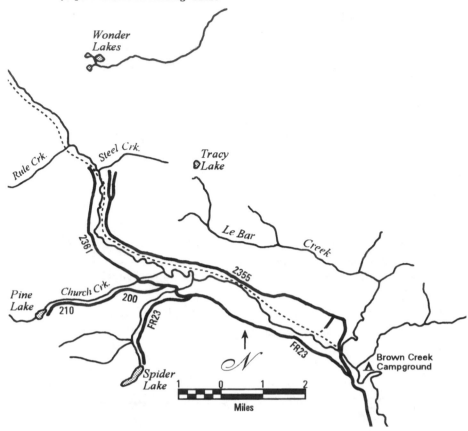

## Spider Lake (1290)

Spider, approximately 23 acres, maximum depth 60 feet, is the headwater of Cedar Creek, draining into the South Fork Skokomish. It is reached by a very complicated route up the maze of logging roads off the South Fork Skokomish Road. This has historically been an eastern brook lake and when it has been overstocked, the fish have resultingly been quite small. Cutthroat naturally reproduce in limited numbers in the outlet to this lake.

## Pine Lake (2,250)

Pine Lake is seven acres, approximately 25 feet deep. Fish do not naturally reproduce in this lake and rainbow and cutthroat are planted regularly. It is reached up the South Fork Skokomish Road, past Brown Creek Campground on FR23, turning left just after passing Cedar Creek, continuing past the first road to the left and straight on to the lake, approximately 3.5 miles.

## Haven Lake (1100)

Heavily planted with rainbow, cutthroat, and even kokanee and sea–run cutthroat on occasion, this 15 acre lake is over 60 feet deep in many places.

Studies found that eastern brook and kokanee naturally reproduce in the inlets to the lake, but rainbow do not. It is reached by driving up the South Fork Skokomish Road to a major intersection just southeast of Camp Govey, turning left and following road #2342 to the outlet of Haven Lake.

## Drybed Lakes

The Drybed Lakes are reached by driving north from Matlock, left on road #2341, then following road #2345 to the lower lake.

*Lower Drybed Lake (1150).* This 7 acre lake is 105 feet deep in the middle. At one time packed with small eastern brook no larger than 7 inches, it is periodically planted with rainbow.

*Upper Drybed Lake (l250).* 5 acres and 35 feet deep, the lake also has historically contained eastern brook no larger than 7 inches and is planted regularly with rainbow.

## Flat Lake (1250)

Flat Lake drains into Flat Creek and Rock Creek, which in turn flow into the South Fork Skokomish River. Consult your map to locate this lake because it is 150 yards off the road and difficult to find. Full of eastern

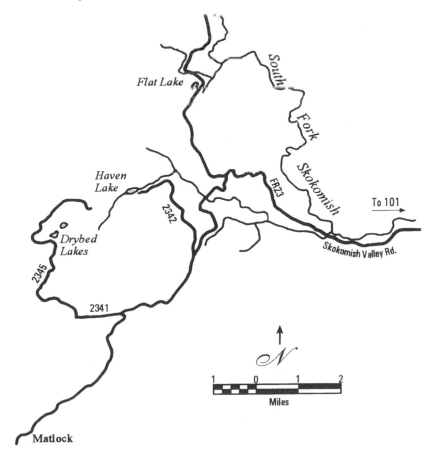

brook, 30 feet deep in the middle, this is a good place for children to learn to fly fish for abundant trout.

## Tracy Lake (4000)

Tracy Lake drains into Steel Creek, which flows into the South Fork Skokomish. It can be reached by hiking cross country from the highest bend of Road #2355 as it parallels Steel Creek, an approximate 1500 foot elevation gain in 2 miles. Map work is required if attempting to reach this lake because the creek disappears approximately a mile below the lake. Long ago stocking was recommended, but there is no indication it has been planted and the existence of trout in the lake is uncertain.

## Wonder Lakes (4000)

Located high in the Wonder Mountain Wilderness area just outside the Park boundary, two of the Wonder Lakes are stocked regularly and are reported to provide very good fishing. Cross–country hiking from the Upper South Fork Skokomish Trail is required, using map and compass.

# Wynoochee

## Wynoochee River

A trip up the Wynoochee River for trout fishing could best be described as a long haul over a rough road for very little in the way of fishing. Above Lake Wynoochee there are no anadromous fish, the river is large enough to hold a decent trout population but there seem to be very few there. There is considerable fishing pressure and this may be the reason.

The area immediately above the lake and for several miles further is flat, open and there are decent sized holes. Upriver from this the river enters more of a canyon like area, with boulders, plunge pools, and good holding water.

Continuing up the Wynoochee Road beyond Wynoochee Falls, the river is accessible by bushwhacking in several places. Here it is truly a beautiful stream but little more than a mountain creek. There are insects and there appears to be plenty of food but still few fish. The holes are deep enough, the water cool enough and there is little explanation for the absence of decent sized trout.

By the time the road crosses the Wynoochee for the final time, it is merely a small creek, not really worth the effort to fish it.

## Satsop Lakes (1500)

Follow FR23 to the right at the junction with the Wynoochee Road and FR22 leading to the left. A sign to the lakes points in the right direction but the sign tends to be on the impermanent side. Then travel on road #2372 to a junction with several logging roads to locate the Satsop Lakes. Consult your map. Satsop Lakes consist of Satsop #1, 8 acres, Satsop #2, 3 acres, also

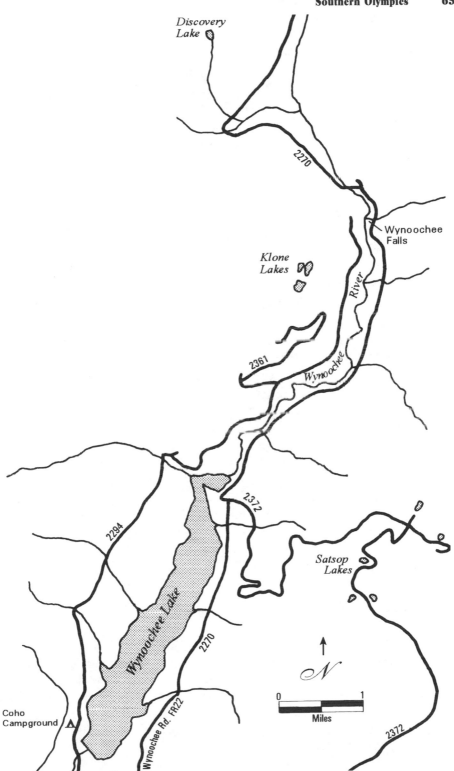

Discovery
Lake

2270

Wynoochee
Falls

Klone
Lakes

River

Wynoochee

2361

2372

2294

Satsop
Lakes

Wynoochee Lake

2270

*N*

0          1
Miles

Coho
Campground

Wynoochee Rd. FR22

2372

known as Spike Lake, Satsop #4, 2 acres, and Satsop #5, 3 acres (the road travels immediately next to this lake).

*Satsop #1.* This lake holds good numbers of brook to 10–12 inches. It is periodically planted with rainbow. They spawn, but it does not appear that they spawn every year. Satsop #1 is 0.25 miles from the road and requires some searching to find. A relatively productive lake, it produces fat, although not especially large, trout.

*Satsop #2.* Eastern brook to 10–11 inches have generally populated this lake with some limited natural spawning. It is planted periodically with rainbow trout as well. It is approximately 300 yards from the road.

*Satsop #3.* Satsop #3 is 1.5 acres and nearly dries up each summer. It does not contain trout.

*Satsop #4.* This lake has historically held eastern brook which reproduce to a limited extent. Satsop #4 is 25 feet from the closest road.

*Satsop #5* is approximately 10 feet deep at its deepest and blocked by a beaver dam. The road passes directly between this lake and a small pond. This logging road apparently bisected the lake since logging debris were left in the lake. Limited natural spawning of eastern brook occurs in Satsop #5.

## Klone Lakes (3175)

Klone Lakes have no established hiking routes to them. They are found off of road #2361 above the Wynoochee River, approximately 4 miles above Wynoochee Lake. If you don't already know how to get there, you will need a detailed contour map to find them.

*Klone #1.* This 9 acre lake is approximately 80 feet deep and is about a 2 hour hike from the nearest road. Long ago it was planted with rainbow, which in limited numbers grew to as big as 20 inches, due to the abundant food in Klone #1.

*Klone #2.* 5 acres and 50 feet deep.

*Klone #3.* Klone #3 is 2 acres and approximately 15 feet deep.

None of these lakes support naturally reproducing trout. They depend upon stocking and certainty regarding the existence of a trout population requires a telephone call to the State of Washington Department of Fish and Wildlife.

## Discovery Lake (3300)

Discovery Lake is the headwater of Discovery Creek and is reported to be accessible by hiking straight up Discovery Creek from Road #2270 after the road crosses the Wynoochee River and branches left about 2 miles above Wynoochee Falls. Follow #2270 until it crosses Discovery Creek. Discovery Lake is 2.5 acres, 15 feet deep. This lake is planted with cutthroat regularly, which are said to grow to very large sizes. To reach this lake requires map, compass and route-finding skills, with an elevation gain of 1800 feet in approximately 1.5 miles.

*Upper Wynoochee River. Author photo.*

*"Fishing isn't what it used to be, and we old timers must needs live in the past, for nowadays, with the legal limit placed at 25, it's the size of the fish and not the number that counts." —E. B. Webster*

# Western Olympics

*"We were at Mr. Morganroth's ranch on the Bogachiel early in 1922. . . .Mr. Morganroth insisted there is no stream in the Olympics to compare to his own river when it comes to trout, and the best method of catching them he said, was to ride a pony out in the water and fish downstream from the pony's back."* —E. B. Webster

As a general rule, it is an unsatisfactory experience trying to fish westside rivers like the Queets, Hoh, Bogachiel, Sol Duc, and Quinault until at least July at the earliest and more likely early August through October. They are simply too large and the fish are spread out until a drop in the water level forces them to concentrate and hang out in holding lies more accessible to anglers.

## Bogachiel

### Bogachiel River

The Bogachiel River, located close to the town of Forks, is quite heavily fished in its lower stretches. The road off Highway 101 extends 5.5 miles up

*Upper Bogachiel River. NPS photo.*

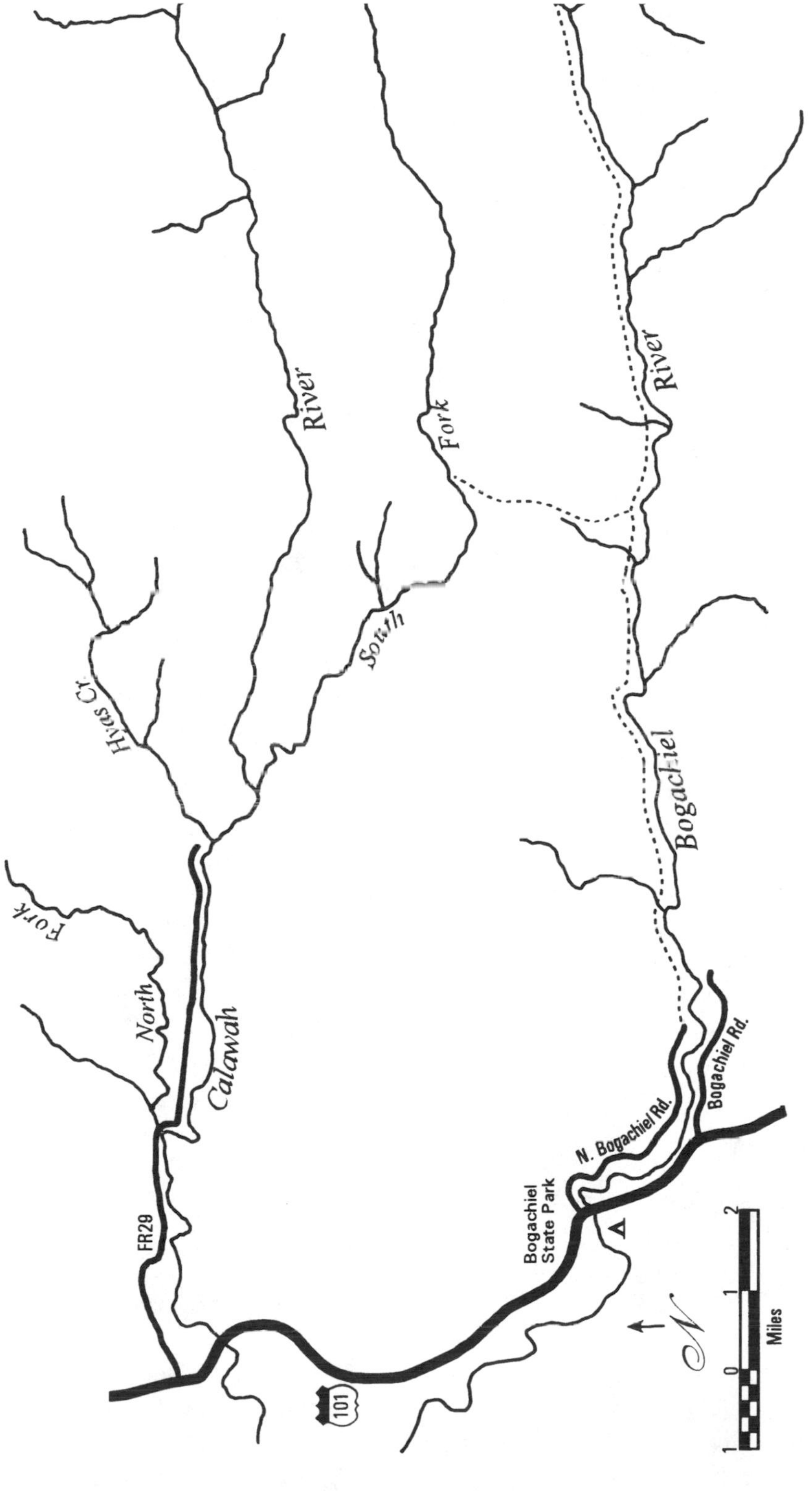
North Fork
Calawah
Hyas Cr.
River
South Fork
Bogachiel River
FR29
101
Bogachiel State Park
N. Bogachiel Rd.
Bogachiel Rd.
N
Miles
1
0
1
2

the river, where the Bogachiel Trail begins. Below the trailhead, there is fishing for small rainbow to 12 inches and occasional steelhead smolt.

A long hike up the Bogachiel Trail, as long as 12–15 miles, brings fishermen to what has been frequently described as excellent rainbow fishing, with fish to 12 inches much more abundant than in the lower river. The fishing is reputedly the best at 15 Mile Camp. A shorter hike of about 8 or 9 miles brings you to the more canyon–like area in the Bogachiel where holding water becomes more consistent and trout fishing is rewarding.

This is a pleasant river to fish, not difficult to wade and worth the effort put into hiking to its upper reaches. It supports rainbow, a few resident cutthroat and eastern brook, Dolly Varden, whitefish, and sizable runs of salmon, steelhead and sea–run cutthroat. Hiking in a distance in the fall may present the opportunity to hook any of the resident fish population and try for returning adult anadromous fish.

## Calawah River

The easiest access to the Calawah is along the road from Forks which follows the river for about 7 miles until just beyond Hyas Creek the road heads uphill to be lost in a maze of logging roads. Above Hyas Creek, the Calawah is called the South Fork.

The river may be fished all along this road to the point where it departs, but it does not appear to hold a substantial number of sizable trout, particularly closer to Forks. The Calawah is very deep in many places, swimming depth, but there is very little fast water and it's a long distance between pools and heads of pools; a lot of walking is required.

The South Fork upstream from where the road leaves the Calawah has potential for good fishing, but again you have to walk quite a distance between good spots to find fish. The river does become a little faster, deeper with more holes with riffles at the head of them.

There is access to the upper South Fork by hiking 6.1 miles on the Bogachiel Trail, then 3.4 miles on the Indian Pass Trail which climbs up over Indian Ridge to the South Fork. There is no means of getting to the upper South Fork by road and few fishermen reach it, but reports of fishing are good.

# *Hoh*

## Hoh River

> *"We had learned there was no fishing in the Hoh, the water being too roily when the river was low. We found a dull gray stream, below the silt–filled surface of which we could not see to the depth of even a half–inch."—E. B. Webster*

The Hoh is a big, often cloudy river and much of the year it cannot be forded safely. At low water the cloudiness diminishes, it is fishable without great difficulty and is crossable.

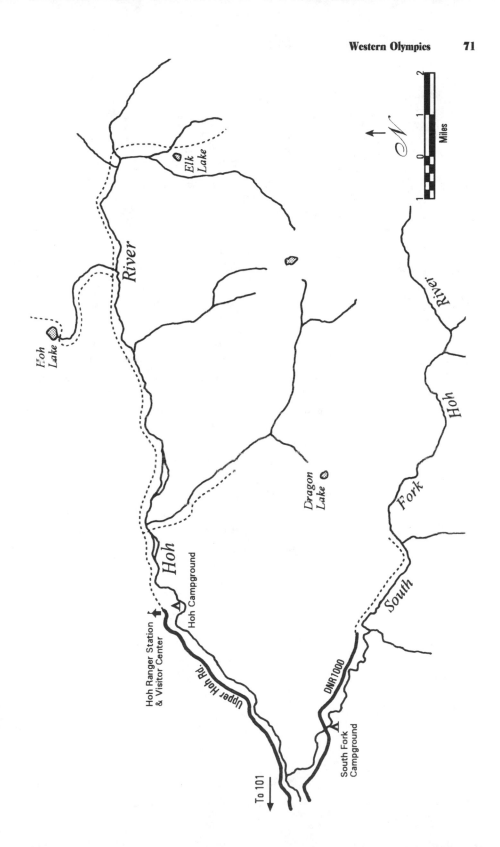

*Hoh River.*
*NPS photo.*

Access is good along the 18.5 mile road to the Hoh visitor station, beginning at Highway 101. There are plenty of 6–12 inch trout and steelhead smolts in the Hoh. There is steady walking between holes, however, and the chance of hooking a large trout here is minimal.

Hoh River trout do not seem to rise to the fly as readily as in some other Olympic rivers, probably because of the milkiness of the water. In general, the higher up the Hoh, the more fishable the water and the less competition from anadromous fish. Still, steelhead smolts will rise to the fly throughout the Hoh and when they are 10–14 inches they make for some of the more exciting river fishing in the Olympics. Whitefish abound and can be caught with small nymphs and wet flies. Fall fishing gives the angler the chance to catch returning salmon, steelhead, sea–run cutthroat and sea–run Dolly Varden in addition to the resident species.

The lower section of the Hoh is too large and the holding spots too poorly defined to comfortably fish for trout.

## South Fork Hoh

The South Fork Hoh Trail begins at the end of DNR Road 1000, 10.4 miles from its origin on the Hoh–Clearwater Road. The trail continues 3.3 miles, mostly along the river, and dedicated fishermen can continue through the woods for more than another mile. Late summer surveys have shown large numbers of trout in the South Fork but a small percentage over 12 inches. It has been placed under catch-and-release rules by the Park Service. There are a few Dolly Varden and the usual large number of whitefish in the South Fork.

## Hoh Lake (4500)

Hoh Lake is more easily reached from the Sol Duc area (see Sol Duc) but may also be hiked to by traveling up the Hoh River Trail 9.5 miles to the

Hoh Lake Trail, which begins at 1000 feet and ends 5.3 miles later at the lake. The lake is of unsurpassed beauty and is worth the hike from either direction.

## Elk Lake (2558)

Hiking 14.6 miles up the mostly flat Hoh River Trail, the last 1.5 miles climb steeply to Elk Lake, which resembles a lowland lake despite being so deep into the Park. Situated in a pocket between Martin and Glacier Creeks, it is 6 acres and produces eastern brook.

## Clearwater River

There is decent seasonal fishing for salmon, steelhead, and sea–run cutthroat in this slow moving river, but little in the way of resident trout.

# Queets

### Queets River

As you drive up the river to the Ranger Station in the Queets Valley, a beautiful 13.6 mile drive, you are inside the park almost immediately after leaving Highway 101. Along the way the road crosses the small Salmon River, possibly worth wading upstream to fish. At the end of the Queets road, one can drop into the river, begin fishing, and work upstream, but it's a long slog between holes in places. The river can be forded and you can hike as many miles as you want up the deeply wooded flat trail to various points on the river.

The Queets holds a good variety of fish: small rainbow, whitefish, a very few resident cutthroat in the higher stretches, and seasonally, sea–run cutthroat, salmon and steelhead. It is best known though for its Dolly

*Queets River whitefish. Author photo.*

Varden. The Park Service has designated the Queets above the Park boundary as catch and release water to provide a quality fishing experience on a wilderness river.

There have been ongoing discussions nationally about bull trout (Dolly Varden) designation as an endangered species. The Park Service recognizes its population of Dolly Varden as increasingly rare and has sought to protect it. Combining this with the fact that sea–run cutthroat and wild summer–run steelhead are also becoming exceedingly rare, catch and release in this area makes excellent sense.

Catching Dolly Varden is another matter, however. They are notoriously reluctant to rise to a dry fly and favor deep slow moving pools, in most instances, except when salmon and steelhead are spawning; then they will move out of their holes to follow them. Dolly Varden in the Queets are reported up to well beyond 20 inches and there are a substantial enough number to make fishing for them a valuable part of your trip. Fly fishermen have the best success using a sink tip, preferably the fastest sinking tip available, because the water does move quickly, with a variety of streamers and nymphs, such as the Bucktail Coachman, Muddler Minnow, other

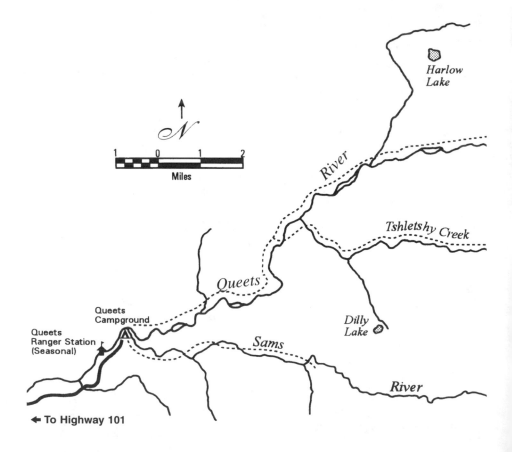

*Queets River. Francis Caldwell photo.*

minnow imitations, and heavy, weighted nymphs.

There are also steelhead in the Queets seasonally and you may hook one of them while fishing for Dollies. Sea–run cutthroat are really only available in the fall and it takes a good deal of hunting to find them, but experienced fishermen who hike up the Queets Trail report excellent fishing for them in the fall, along with Dollies, an occasional steelhead and even salmon once in a while. The Queets is not good dry fly water, except perhaps just before dark when you see occasional fish rising.

The upper Queets offers the best fishing and is well worth a two or three day trip.

## Tshletshy Creek

This creek, about halfway up the Queets Trail, is so named for the local Native American word for "halfway." It is reached by hiking up the Queets Trail 5.6 miles to a fork in the trail leading to Tshletshy Creek, 0.8 miles. There is reputedly good fishing for resident trout in this moderate sized stream.

## Sams River

The Sams River Trail begins at the end of Queets River Road and allows access to this small river, which produces anadromous fish and small trout.

# *Quinault*

## Quinault River and North Fork Quinault River

Above Lake Quinault the Quinault River is accessible both from the North Shore and South Shore roads. Be sure to check at the ranger station for the possibility of a road being washed out. The river is large and has substantial numbers of small rainbow, the occasional larger rainbow and steelhead smolt to 12 inches and slightly larger.

Approximately 8 miles up the road from Lake Quinault Lodge, the North Fork flows in above a bridge to the left, which in turn leads to the North Fork Trail. The North Fork is a medium size river almost perfect for fly fishing. Its lower stretch, from the bridge across the North Fork to the beginning of the trailhead, contains a variety of habitat, including long, shoulder deep pools, riffles, boulder water and also, unfortunately, a few long empty stretches of shallow water. Nevertheless, this river is very much worth fishing as it contains rainbow and immature steelhead to 12 inches and bigger. It also has a few Dolly Varden and large numbers of whitefish. It is easily accessible by a short slog through the woods from the road.

The larger North Fork steelhead smolt fight very hard, jump like miniature steelhead, make powerful runs and will break you off using 6x. How do you know whether you have a steelhead smolt or resident rainbow? "Indeed," says Dr. Jordan in his *Trout of the West*, "the keen discernment of a magician is required to distinguish the Steelhead from the Rainbow. . .God never made a harder fighting fish." One sage fisherman observed that if you have a 10 inch fish that fights ridiculously hard it is probably a steelhead smolt. This seems doubly so for a 12–14 incher. That is not to say that rainbow don't fight hard, but it may be that this is the best way to tell. This

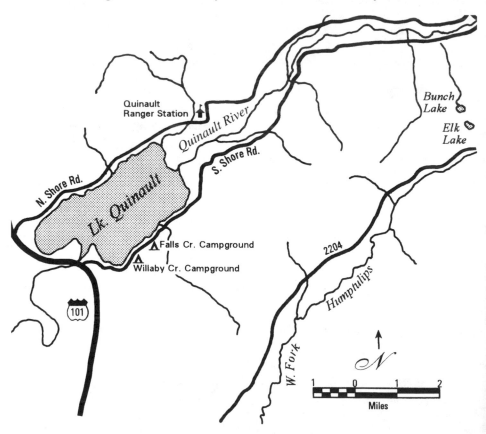

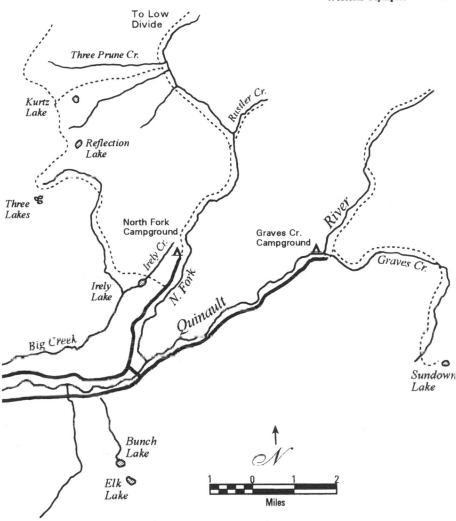

kind of excitement is not often found trout fishing in the Olympics and it is not the norm on the North Fork, but is available.

Above the North Fork trailhead, it is possible to hike beyond the reach of all but the most courageous anadromous fish, and very good fishing with numerous trout in the 12 inch range is reported up approximately 8 miles and further. Eventually, the river gets too small to fish, but anywhere above the trailhead seems to provide decent fishing. Surveys in the North Fork from Wolf Bar downstream have shown trout, over 12 inches, although not especially numerous, to comprise about 1/4 of the trout population in some sections.

The main stem Quinault above the North Fork is commonly called the East Fork and there is plenty of fishing access off the road which follows it another 6.3 miles to Graves Creek and Enchanted Valley trailheads. There are at least 15 miles of the Enchanted Valley Trail which parallel the river and fishing opportunities are unlimited. Surveys indicate predominately small rainbow trout, large numbers of whitefish, some Dolly Varden and eastern brook in the river.

## Sundown Lake (3900)

0.1 miles up the Enchanted Valley Trail, the Graves Creek Trail leads 6.6 miles to a 1 mile way trail to Sundown Lake. It is 3 acres, oval shaped and perhaps 50 feet deep. It has periodically been barren but it appears possibly capable of limited spawning. Rainbow were planted in it long ago and trout found in it would be the progeny of those plantings.

## Irely Lake (600)

Shortly before the end of the North Fork Road, the Big Creek Trail leads a pleasant 1 mile to Irely Lake, which is somewhat remarkable in that it is found in a lowland area which appears to have once not had a lake in it, then to have had a sizable lake which now seems to dry up and shrink to about 1 acre at low water in the fall. The Park Service has imposed special regulations and it is presently catch-and-release. It has historically held brook, native cutthroat and rainbow, with fish reaching nearly two pounds. It is sometimes overpopulated with 100's of 3–5 inch fish but there are still good sized trout in this lake.

The lake is fishable from opening day to the last day of the season by which time it can become nothing more than a small pond. Early fishing is best, as most of the larger fish appear to retreat from the lake into its source stream as the lake decreases its size through summer. By late summer, much of what was lake bottom in spring, becomes a byway for deer and elk. A trip here at dawn or just before dark might be memorable for the number of animals sighted.

*Irely Lake in Spring. John Meyer photo.*

*Irely Lake in Fall. Author photo.*

The lake has natural spawning in its inlet and outlet and is self–sustaining. The Park Service believes it to be the only lake within the Park which had a native population of cutthroat before stocking occurred.

### Three Lakes (3400)

By continuing beyond Irely Lake another 4.7 miles, at the junction of the Skyline and Tshletshy Creek Trails, Three Lakes are reached, all approximately one acre. The largest lake contains eastern brook.

### Reflection Lake (3550)

A hike of another 2.9 miles brings you to one acre Reflection Lake, headwater to Big Creek. This long shallow lake, located in a high glacial pocket, is about 0.25 miles east of the Skyline Trail and difficult to see. It contains eastern brook.

### Kurtz Lake (4000)

Beyond Reflection Lake, approximately 2 miles, the trail forks to the right to Kurtz Lake, barely one acre which flows into Three Prune Creek, reached off the Skyline Ridge Trail which begins near Three Legs Camp. Kurtz lies cross–country to the south and to the southeast, approximately 0.25 miles. There are no known reports of trout.

# *Humptulips*

## Humptulips River

The Humptulips is primarily an anadromous fish system. There are several forks which are also anadromous fish streams but may be worth exploring. Stevens Creek, flowing into the Humptulips just north of the Humptulips settlement has been surveyed and found to support good numbers of trout.

# Bunch Lake (3000) and Elk Lake (3000)

Both lakes are reached by driving up the Humptulips Road then via logging roads on Forest Service land in the area of the headwaters of the Humptulips River. Many of these roads have been subject to conservation closures. Check with Quinault District office of Olympic National Forest for current information. Elk Lake, 11 acres, found in a glacial cirque, is about 1 mile west, cross country. Bunch Lake, 16 acres, is another 0.5 miles northwest of Elk, in a canyon above the lower Quinault River. Both have been reported to hold rainbow, but there appears to be no stream for spawning and the lakes may both be barren.

*"The trials of angling are anticipation and solitude," says Griswold. "It cultivates a habit of observation which is so necessary if one would enjoy a life in nature, and it takes one to beautiful rivers at nature's most attractive season when there is so much that is interesting to observe in both bird and plant life." —E. B Webster.*

# Fishing Techniques

## *Fly Fishing Olympic Mountain Lakes*

### Selecting a Lake

In selecting a lake, consult this guidebook to determine access and what you are likely to catch. Consider also whether the lake is easy or nearly impossible to fish, as some mountain lakes are extremely challenging to fish without a float tube or boat. All of the lakes listed can be fished successfully with flies, but bringing a spin outfit along may be very helpful, particularly for novice anglers.

### Fishing Gear

The primary consideration for fishermen who are hiking is the weight of the gear they will pack in. While hiking, many wear a fishing vest, which contains all necessary (and unnecessary) fishing gear. This gives a slight amount of weight forward on the body and tends to balance the pack a bit. It also allows them to be ready to fish if they find a likely spot on the way to their primary destination.

The most difficult decision involves a rod. There are presently many 4 and 5-piece pack rods available, some for a reasonable price. Most of these fly rods can also be used as spinning rods, although with some degree of difficulty. The problem with most of them is that they are not long enough to allow the shore–bound fly fisherman the necessary distance in casting to get a fly out far enough. An easy solution is to carry a 2–piece 9 foot rod in an aluminum rod case, which is also used as a staff along the trail. Be sure that the rod is carefully padded on either end to avoid too much shock to the tip and ferrule end.

Any reasonable fly reel will do and it is best to have a fly line in the light category, 4–5, as long as you can cast it a long way. Careful and delicate presentations are crucial in mountain lakes because the trout are so easily spooked in the generally crystal clear waters.

Leaders should be as fine and long as possible. A leader of at least 12

*Cedar Lake. NPS photo.*

feet is almost mandatory on many mountain lakes. The only limitation on length is related to whether you can effectively cast the fly with such a long leader. 6X and 7X leaders are recommended, as you will generally be using very small flies and visibility is always an issue.

An inflatable raft or float tube will be very helpful in fishing the lakes because so many of the fish seem to feed just out of casting reach. Whether you want to haul a boat, raft or a float tube depends on how much effort you are willing to put into this hike. It is not generally crucial to your fishing success to have a boat or a float tube, but it is certainly likely that it will improve your results. Some fishermen bring ultralight waders, which pack easily, allow better access to lakes and more effective casting.

Because so many of them have such precipitous shorelines, are heavily treed, may be swampy, and for any number of other reasons, many mountain lakes are very difficult to fish by traditional fly casting. Because of this, it is recommended that the fly fisherman bring an ultralight spinning reel. It is not difficult to fish with a couple of split shot and a wet fly or the old bubble and fly technique. If you bring children on your trip, a spinning reel is almost a necessity for them to have any fishing success. There are exceptions where kids can easily cast flies with a fly line and fly rod, but much of the time that is impossible for them.

## When to Fish

Fishing regulations obviously determine the season, but to have the most effective fishing, there are a number of factors. Most alpine lake fishermen don't begin hiking into lakes to fish until the beginning of July; however, different years have different ice–out times, and consulting the Forest Service and the Park Service is usually the best way to get the right information. The low altitude lakes are nearly always ice-free by opening day, generally the end of the third week in April. By July some high lakes may still be partially iced–over, and others, depending on the amount of exposure to sunlight, will be ice–free. Some may be frozen solid until August.

If the angler is fortunate to fish a lake just at ice–out, the trout will usually be found to be hungry and fishing can be very fast. Once the ice is off the lakes, fishing is best in the morning and particularly in the evening. Fishing is also effective when there are shadows on the lake, for fish seem to feed more actively and feel protected in the shade. If it is breezy, one can usually fish all day with success. Cloudy days provide slightly easier fishing than the brilliant sunny days, when it is best to let the fish nap during midday and do all of the things that are so enjoyable at high mountain lakes.

Any time trout are rising with consistency is also a good time to fish. You can simply cast your dry fly out as far as possible, settle back against a rock or tree, take the slack out of the leader, sit back and wait. Mountain trout, even though not feeding actively, cruise the lake and will often opportunistically take a fly sitting on the surface. You have to be patient, but this is not difficult on a mountain lake, with spectacular scenery, and the need for a good nap.

Other than at ice–out time, fall tends to be the very best time to fish, as temperatures drop and the fish begin to feed to prepare for the winter. At this time of year, especially after school has opened, there are seldom any other hikers, or other fishermen around, and those trout which have managed to elude any fishermen during the summer become less wary. This is often the best opportunity to catch the biggest fish.

## The Best Fishing Locations

Trout circulate around lakes by cruising, often within feet of the shoreline. In the mornings and evenings they will come into the shallow areas, but

*Three Lakes. Francis Caldwell photo.*

avoid them during much of the daytime. If there is an inlet creek, this is often the best place to fish, as trout tend to hang slightly off the current, or just below it. Outlets will also contain fish, particularly those with some depth and flow. Some lakes have undercut banks, where fish like to cruise along underneath, obtaining good cover and a good view of insects coming off the bank.

The zones between the shallow and deep water are often the most productive areas in lakes because they offer the safety of deeper water and the food supply of shallow water. Deep water is difficult to fish, particularly from shore, and fish do not generally feed in deep water. However, there are exceptions, and particularly during the middle of the day, fishing deep is sometimes a necessity. Weed beds, where they exist, often produce the largest number of insects, and fish will hang off of weed beds. Typically, one will have to fish weed beds with dry flies because of the difficulty of getting a nymph or a wet fly down into the weeds. Log jams, submerged logs, rock piles on the bottom, and any other type of cover in the shallow to deep water zone provide good cover for trout. Finally, some lakes have springs, where trout like to hang out.

Approach a mountain lake as quietly and carefully as possible. You will quickly realize how incredibly still the environment is, and if the wind is not blowing, how still the surface of the lake is as well. If you see trout rising within casting distance, go ahead and fish to them. If not, look for an inlet or outlet stream and consider whether you want to thrash through the woods or across the rocks to get there. It will usually be worth it to get to an inlet stream. Otherwise, your decision about where to fish will be based primarily upon whether you can reach the fish by casting from any particular spot. If you can only cast to very shallow water, it is unlikely that spot will be worth it. More importantly, can you backcast? More often than not you cannot backcast around much of the lake shore.

*Lake Angeles. NPS photo.*

You may decide to simply

*Upper Elk Lake cutthroat. Author photo.*

circle the lake, casting as you move around it. If so, exercise great care because mountain lake shorelines are extremely fragile and degrade easily. Remember that fish generally circulate around the shoreline and will ultimately come to you, with some exceptions, such as inlets, springs, and weed beds where fish are inclined to remain for significant periods of time. Logs which stick out into the lake may be your first point of entry to cast, but be careful—they are slippery and sometimes they will sink right under you. Points are often the best because you can cast straight out and both left and right without hanging up your backcast.

Finally, be aware of the importance of wind direction. If nothing else the wind will allow you to get your cast out further if it's at your back. A continuous strong wind tends to pile up insects at the downwind part of a lake. If you are a strong caster, you may wish to locate yourself at the end of the lake where the wind is blowing everything and cast into the breeze. You will often find fish waiting there to feed on insects which are blown down to that end of the lake. Conversely, sometimes the fish will be at that end of the shore where the wind is blowing insects off trees and bushes into the lake. This is particularly true with ant hatches; if you find such a hatch, it is likely to provide you with the best lake fishing of any kind, for fish go absolutely berserk in their feeding on the ants.

## Technique

Once you've selected a spot to begin fishing, note that the clarity of the water is almost always perfect and anything that lands upon the lake surface can also be seen. Ideally, fishermen will learn to follow E. B. Webster's dictum, "the art of skimming the flies out over the water so they will settle as softly as thistle seed."

Your decision to fish on top or below the surface comes next. If fish are rising, first attempt to determine what family of fly is on the surface. If that is impossible, start with a small Adams and change, if necessary. Your cast must be very smooth and very delicate. After the fly lands on the surface, tighten the line to straighten the leader and wait. There are high lake fishermen who straighten the leader, take out a book and start reading, those who begin eating, and those who sit and simply contemplate their surroundings. If fish are rising consistently, it is probable that eventually a fish will take your dry fly. Patience is truly a virtue in dry fly fishing high mountain lakes because every time you lift your line off, every false cast, and every time you drop the line on the water tends to disturb the fish at least momentarily.

*Royal Lake. NPS photo.*

When fish continue to rise, and will simply not take anything offered, switch to the corresponding nymph, fished either in the surface film of the lake or just below. Slight movement and a variety of retrieves is appropriate to represent the emerging stage of the fly, but seldom is much movement needed. Lifting the rod occasionally to cause your nymph to rise, then dead drifting is sometimes a useful technique.

If no fish are rising, you probably will not want to fish with a dry fly. A good idea when nothing is rising is to sample the shoreline, to see if you can determine what is moving about in the water, attempt to find an imitation for it and start with a nymph or wet fly. As a general rule, nymphs and wet flies need not be fished terribly deep, except perhaps in the middle of the day. Water temperature during the hottest part of the summer may make a difference, but usually the clarity of the water is such that fish can see your moving nymph from a very long distance away. If nothing works below the surface or halfway down, you will simply have to get down to the bottom. Use a floating line with either a heavily–weighted nymph, or an attractor such as a woolly bugger or muddler, fished with a shot slightly above it, or fish a fast–sinking line.

If you are shore–bound and simply unable to get the fly out into the lake because of impossible casting situations, try a spinning reel with a bubble and fly. Casting bubbles are approximately 1–1.5 inches in diameter and come in a variety of sizes. You can add weight to them by adding shot right below the bubble but usually they are heavy enough to throw a fly a long distance. It is recommended that you use approximately four to 6 feet of 6X or 5X leader beyond the bubble, to the fly. As with fly line fishing, once the bubble hits the water, tighten up and let it sit. If you are fishing it with a nymph, give it only very slight movement and work it back.

If the bubble and fly technique does not work, and you have children along, you may wish to use spoons and even bait, if necessary and regulations allow, to keep them interested.

When fishing from a float tube or a boat, high mountain lakes are so still and the water so clear that you must put an extraordinary distance between yourself and the fly, at least 60 feet and preferably 75–100 feet.

Many high lake fishermen use droppers, a system of two or three flies on the same leader, tied approximately 12–18 inches apart. This is an effective way to fish.

One should always use barbless hooks. Not only is fish mortality reduced, but so is flesh mortality, for sooner or later all fishermen are going to hook themselves, sometimes with the hook going clear in past the barb. You'll find pulling that hook out to be a lot easier without a barb on it.

## Eight Dependable Flies

Nearly every fly fisherman carries perhaps 50–100 or more flies on a fishing trip. The amount time spent changing flies is often wasted. The flies listed here will give you the basic eight, which you need and can use effectively:

     1. *Adams*—20 through 12.
     2. *Scud* — 18 through 12, in a variety of colors, tan preferred.
     3. *Callibaetis Nymph*—18 through 14.
     4. *Chironomid Nymph*— 18 though 10, in red, brown, black, tan and olive.
     5. *Hare's Ear*—18–10.
     6. *Midge*— 22–16 in black and gray.
     7. *Pheasant Tail*— 18–14.
     8. **Woo**lly **Bugger**—12–6 in black, tan, olive and brown.

Soft hackles in a variety of colors and sizes are useful all–purpose flies and will often work with a variety of retrieves.

# Fly Fishing
# Olympic Mountain Streams

## Spring Runoff

Regulations prohibit trout fishing in nearly all Olympic streams until late spring at the earliest. All of the rivers and creeks are subject to heavy spring flows, which often cause muddy water, but not always. If the color of the river is chocolate brown, forget about fishing. If it is clear, though, it is fishable, mostly around the edges. You'll be pleasantly surprised how active the fish can be once the water temperature warms during runoff.

## Subsiding Runoff/Summer

As summer comes on, temperatures continue to warm, streams clear, and insects renew their life cycle. If you find a stream that is still swollen but is clear along the edges, give it a try. The fish tend to hang off the main flow, and you should look to the edges where the insects migrate, get loose from their holds; it is time for the fish to feed.

Once summer is underway, the streams gradually reduce to normal flow, clarity returns to most, with some exceptions, and fish are spread throughout the river, taking holding and feeding lies, which are familiar to all fly fishermen.

Occasionally during the summer, there will be a heavy rainfall. While this may color the river, again look toward the banks and holding spots close by. The fish will be there.

## Fall

As the days grow shorter, trout often feed more avidly. Water temperatures drop and the best fishing will usually be during the warmth of the

*North Fork Quinault River rainbow. Author photo.*

*Upper
Dungeness
River.
Author
photo.*

middle of the day. Fish gradually move away from their feeding stations toward the pools.

Trout fishing is generally at its best in July, August and September in the Olympics, but early October can be good as well. With the passing of summer, the streams shrink in size and every hole seems accessible.

Finally, the leaves begin to fall, and often so many drop into the rivers of the Olympics that fishing is almost impossible with both wet and dry flies. Don't give up, because fish can be caught even on days when leaves are streaming down the surface of the water, and many are sunken and rushing along as well. The fish are still feeding, and it is just a matter of adjusting your technique. Sometimes you have to wait until leaves go by and fish the gap, and other times you will find that leaves stay in a particular part of the current and fish will move to the side.

## Equipment

> *"You meet George out on the Elwha and like as not you will find him using a crooked alder pole, his reel seated with a turn or two of adhesive tape, and for flies one or two professors or hackles." —E. B. Webster*

An 8 1/2–9 foot 4 or 5 weight rod is ideal for the Olympic streams. Some smaller waters may justify going down to 8 feet, but it is not recommended that you go any smaller. Reaching, dapping, and fishing with just a small amount of fly line out beyond the rod tip is a common technique on Olympic streams and much easier when using a 9 foot rod. You will not need to make long sweeping backcasts or get a lot of line out.

Regarding leader length, in dry fly fishing, there seem to be two schools of thought. One asserts that on small streams and creeks, use no longer than a 7–9 foot leader. This is fine if you can control the fly's drift with that length of leader and it is unlikely to spook fish, but the number of cross–currents, rocks, and other difficulties encountered in keeping a dry fly where you want it for any length of time suggests adopting the other view: the use of a longer leader, preferably at least ten to twelve feet, depending upon the skill of the angler. The more leader there is on the water, the longer the drift without drag.

For subsurface fishing a 6–7 foot leader is generally better, although the type of water you will find is usually fast, roiled with cross–currents and eddies which will pick up a fly quickly if you have a very short leader. A longer leader allows a longer drift but throwing a weighted fly on a 10–12 foot leader is extremely difficult when you are not using much fly line. Dapping with a longer leader is easier and so is dropping a nymph behind boulders and into small pockets, particularly if you use a weighted fly. Experimentation is necessary to develop the most effective technique.

The size of trout in Olympic rivers justifies a very fine tippet in nearly all situations. You will fish more effectively with it, it will be more of a challenge to land trout and you won't be derricking as many fish up over your shoulder onto the bank when surprised by strikes. 6X is recommended for all dry fly fishing and 4X for wet fly and nymph fishing.

*Upper Sol Duc River cutthroat. Author photo.*

# Fly Types

> *"I will herewith set forth my idea as to the proper assortment for a day's fishing in the Olympic Mountain streams: First, you should select six brown hackles; then add three coachmen, three professors, and six brown hackles." E.B Webster*

**Dry Flies.** If you are a dry fly fisherman and what excites you most is seeing trout rise, the Olympic streams will be just fine with you as long as

*Gray Wolf River. Author photo.*

fish size doesn't matter too much. On a good day in late summer, you might have as many as 50–100 fish rise to your fly in 3–4 hours. There are a few fundamental rules:

You will seldom find a really significant hatch on an Olympic stream. There will be hatches, but they are usually short and there will be a lot fewer insects than you would see in the rivers of Montana or Idaho. Even if you are lucky enough to find a hatch, usually you can match it easily enough with an Adams or an Elk Hair Caddis. The absence of frequent hatches does not mean that the trout will not take dry flies. Quite the contrary. It is a rare day that you cannot catch Olympic trout on a dry fly, perhaps because food is limited and the competition for it is intense.

The Adams is far and away the most important mayfly in these streams. Other useful mayflies include an occasional March Brown and the Royal Family of flies, Royal Coachman, Royal Wulf, and Royal Trude.

For caddis flies, nothing can beat the Elk Hair Caddis. Even when there are no caddis showing, it is an unusual day when the Elk Hair cannot cause Olympic trout to rise. Sometimes, only the smallest ones will rise, but eventually the largest will come up for it as well.

You do not need very many of each type of fly, i.e., two or three types of mayflies, one or two types of caddis, and some terrestrials, perhaps a stone fly.

More trout may rise to a size 14 dry fly but a 12 is a better choice. A 10 is usually too big and a 16 is either tough to keep floating or hard to see. It is suggested that you start with a 12 but be ready immediately to go to a 14 and even a 16. A 12 is much easier to fish, much more visible and it is more likely that larger trout will come after it rather than a 14 or 16.

Olympic trout are not selectively feeding on size 20 midges or baetis microflies and are instead looking for a meal. The larger trout are often looking for the larger meal. The 12s also help keep the pesky 3 and 4 inchers off, when the 14 will not.

A good floatant is essential on all Olympic streams as they are fast moving and riffly.

*"Did you ever see a box of dry flies? They are the tiniest little things, the brightest colored, the most natural, most exquisite . . . they are almost priceless." —E.B. Webster*

*Sol Duc cutthroat caught with Elk Hair Caddis. Author photo.*

***Nymphs, Wet Flies and Streamers***. The general idea with nymphs and wet flies is that when trout will not take anything on top, you will have to fish underneath, and also that larger trout are caught with nymphs, wet flies and streamers. This is no doubt true in many rivers, particularly those of substantial size, but does not seem to be so in the Olympic streams. For one thing, the depth of most streams is not prohibitive for trout to expend the energy to rise to a dry fly.

Nevertheless, there will be times, particularly in the spring during runoff and warming times, and again in the fall, when wet flies, nymphs and streamers will be very useful. Hare's Ears, Zug Bugs, and Caddis Pupa are effective patterns. Weighted nymphs are best, because they can easily be dropped into pockets and riffles. There is not much sink time in fast Olympic rivers and they must get down quickly. Strike indicators are helpful but not absolutely essential.

Soft hackle flies are probably the most useful and easily fished of all wet flies. You can search the stream with them, they will sometimes be taken dead drift, but most frequently as they swing across the current, resembling the emerging form. This is simple fishing and a good way to teach beginning anglers. If all else fails, try Webster's favorite, the Brown Hackle.

*Whitefish.* Virtually all of the westside rivers have more whitefish than trout and there are populations in many of the other Olympic streams. Whitefish are far more reluctant than trout to rise to dry flies, but at times will go on surface feeding sprees and are the only fish which can be caught. Despite being denigrated by most fishermen, they fight well, though they almost never jump. Nymphs, streamers, and wet flies, all in small sizes, will take whitefish, adding pleasure to a fishing trip when trout action is slow.

## Approaching the Fish

Approach cautiously, move slowly, fish quietly upstream, and avoid alerting the small fish at the tail end of good holding areas. Once a fish or two have been taken out of a particular hole, wade on up because there are bound to be lots of good spots upstream. While there are streams that call for a long walk between holding areas, this is usually not the case. Keep moving and you will find fishing to be more productive.

Wading is very helpful, if not essential in all Olympic streams. There are too many bushes, boulders and trees on the banks to move up the river and cast comfortably without wading. It will seldom be necessary to ford a river; do it only when it can be done safely. Don't endanger yourself for a really great looking hole. It is unlikely that such spots will hold fish much larger than the ones you will catch in riffles, pockets and other likely spots reachable from a safe position.

Hipboots are not recommended except for the small streams and a few of the smaller rivers because you occasionally need to go up to your hips to fish effectively. You will inevitably fall in, and filling up your hip boots is not one of the day's highlights, as well as sometimes presenting a serious danger.

Featherweight waders are strongly recommended because they can be

*Olympic Mountain alpine creek. Francis Caldwell photo.*

carried along so easily on short walks to streams and pack nicely for even the longest hike. A pair of featherweights can really make the difference between poor fishing and good fishing because they enable the angler to reach most of the good spots on the stream and allow fording when necessary.

# Spin Fishing

Spin fishing, when certain practices are followed, is very much a low–impact and effective way to fish the Olympic streams and lakes. Never use triple or double hook lures—they are too hard on fish and cause an unacceptable mortality rate. There is also a tendency in spin fishing to horse fish out of the water, including reeling them right up to the rod tip. The use of reasonable drag and care of fish is essential.

Spin fishing can be particularly effective in streams when they are still running rather full and are cloudy. Many lakes are much more easily fished by spin casting than fly rod casting, particulary those with heavily vegetated shorelines or shallow bottoms extending far out from shore.

Ultralight or light spinning reels and rods are sufficient for Olympic trout. Four pound test line is plenty strong, 3 pound test line is even better on the reel, and works well as leader.

For fishing flies with spinning gear, the spin angler should have a few casting bubbles, the dry flies, wet flies and nymphs recommended in this book, some split shot in a variety of sizes, and some fly floatant for bubble and dry fly fishing.

Spin fishermen have a vast array of lures available. A few suggestions, particularly for lakes, are single hook flatfish, and triple teasers, dick nite, brass spoons for brookie lakes and small Canadian wonderspoons, all of

*Olympic Mountain lake spin fishing. NPS photo.*

which come with single hooks. Others, which generally have to be converted from triple or double to single hook lures, are roostertails, mepps and daredevils.

Spinners work better in streams and spoons are more effective in lakes. Across, down and back spin fishing is usually the most efficient method in streams and getting near the bottom is important. Varying retrieves is important in lakes.

# Additional Recommended Olympic Peninsula Lowland Lakes

### Northern Olympics
Anderson Lake, Crocker Lake, Ludlow Lake, Lost Lake, and Tarboo Lake in the Quilcene/Port Townsend area. Lake Sutherland 15 minutes west of Port Angles.

### Western Olympics
Beaver Lake, near Sappho.

### South Olympics
Wynoochee Reservoir.

### Eastern Olympics
Carson Lake 3 miles from Union on Hood Canal. Spencer Lake near Shelton.

# Olympic Mountain Trout

There are 4 species of "trout" in the Olympic Mountains. Rainbow and cutthroat are true trout, and Dolly Varden and brook are actually chars. Whitefish are also widespread and are related to the salmonoids. The following drawings of trout are supplied courtesy of Stan Jones Publishing, and the drawing of the whitefish was done by Jim Singer.

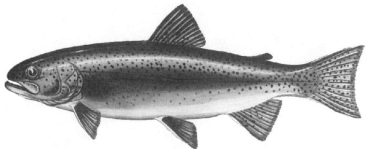

**Rainbow Trout**

## Cutthroat Trout

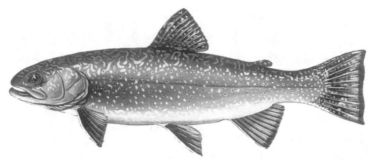

## Brook Trout

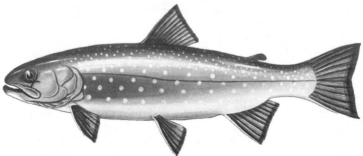

## Dolly Varden

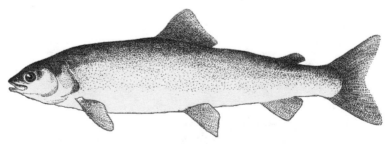

## Whitefish

# Appendix

## Olympic National Park
## Fisheries Management Policy

Recreational fishing as a means of providing enjoyment of the National Parks, has been permitted since 1872. It is managed to assure that overall Park goals are achieved. The Park Service has the authority to restrict recreational fishing whenever necessary to achieve management objectives outlined in Park resource management plans. The primary goal in recreational fisheries management is to maintain a "naturally functioning aquatic ecosystem, protect and perpetuate native aquatic species and natural habitats, and allow recreational fishing activities only when ecosystem impacts are minimal. Beyond ecosystem concerns, management emphasis should be based upon the recreational fishing experience and preservation of the opportunity for fishermen to enjoy the natural aquatic environment, not on fish harvest. Catch–and–release–only regulations should be considered by superintendents, whenever implementation is feasible, to minimize alteration of natural ecological processes. Area zoning is encouraged to provide a choice of catch and release, fly fishing, artificial lure, and/or limited harvest, as well as to avoid gear conflicts."

In keeping with these goals, there is no stocking of fish, naturally fish free waters are not considered "barren," and it is recognized that their condition can be significantly altered by the introduction of fish. Olympic National Park faces a dilemma regarding introduced species, particularly eastern brook. Long ago introduced, this species—actually a char, not a trout—is considered an exotic species, not part of the natural ecosystem. In theory, any lake or stream which contains eastern brook presents a management problem. Regulations direct the superintendent to give high priority to the management and control of exotic fish species that have substantial impact on native fish and associated organisms. Presently the Park has no plans for eradication of any historically introduced population of trout or eastern brook, but remains concerned about their impacts on native fauna.

Olympic National Park also has to pay special attention to anadromous fish, which spend a substantial portion of their life cycle within Park boundaries. Season restrictions, size limits, catch and release regulations, all combine to assure natural reproduction, continuation of those natural processes to which anadromous fish contribute, survival of native species, and quality recreational fishing experiences.

Concerning harvest of fish, the management goal is to determine an optimum harvest level based upon biological balance and integrity as well as the quality of the fishing experience. Consideration is given to adverse impacts from fishing activity upon other resources, such as trampling vegetation, compaction of soil, and disturbance of sensitive wildlife. Possible genetic alteration of species and disruption of spawning activities are given significant weight. Managers are also directed to consider the establishment of restricted waters in which no fishing is allowed, if necessary.

All anglers should appreciate and support Olympic National Park fisheries management policies. Not only do they go far to assure the preservation of one of the last remaining naturally functioning environments, the park also provides quality fishing opportunities and will continue to do so for the future.

# *Regulations*

Anglers using this guide must be aware of the many regulations of the National Park Service, National Forest Service, and Washington Department of Fish & Wildlife controlling entry into and use of the lands of the Olympic Mountains. They must also practice what is commonly called "no trace ethics" to protect the pristine condition of the Olympic environment. Failure to do so harms not only the wilderness ecosystem vital to the integrity of the planet but will cause restrictions in use to be necessitated, limiting areas and opportunities for good future angling experiences.

Every year the Forest Service and Park Service close or restrict use of trails, campsites and even entire areas due to overuse and failure to follow regulations and the no–trace ethic. Anglers in particular have been responsible for degradation of lake and stream shorelines, pollution of waters, short–cutting of trails, trampling of vegetation and a variety of other violations. Deliberate or careless, such practices can only result in needless impacts to resources, expense to the governmental agencies, and restricted use. *Follow regulations carefully and use no–trace ethics. Regulations are subject to change and current regulations must be obtained.*

## No–Trace Hiking, Camping and Fishing

There are many books explaining how to hike, camp and fish with the minimum impact possible. Following regulations to the letter will help a great deal but adopting a no–trace ethic will ensure the minimum impact.

*Hiking.* Stick to the trail except when absolutely no other alternative exists, no short–cutting, no litter, travel in small groups. If cross–country travel is necessary, plan the route well in advance using established way trails whenever possible, stay on solid ground and off fragile vegetation, stay out of stream beds if possible.

*Camping.* Set up only in established campsites. Consult regulations carefully. If no established campsites are available, camp on resilient vegetation and seek bare ground, snow fields, or river gravel bars. Wash cooking and eating equipment at least 100 feet from lakes and streams, avoid using soap. Never bathe in lakes or streams. Do not build campfires unless necessary. Do all cooking with stoves, not campfires. Use only existing fire rings, do not leave fires unattended, extinguish to the point of cold ashes, scatter them and return the ring to its prior condition. Bury all human waste 4–6 inches deep as far away from campsites and water as possible (at least 100 feet). Leave campsites in as natural condition as possible, pack out any trash. Leave no trace.

*Fishing.* Do not damage lake and stream shorelines. Stay on established paths. Pack out any leader or line remnants. Do not use foam strike indicators. Never fish or disturb spawning areas, using particular care in stream spawning areas used by lake trout. Always use barbless hooks. Practice catch and release and follow regulations carefully. If catching fish to eat, burn or bury innards far from shorelines.

# Fishing Regulations and Licenses

Olympic National Park has no license requirement but a variety of regulations, many of which change periodically as a result of Park Service studies and intensity of use. The regulations are available at all visitor entrances and specific regulations are posted at trailheads. There are very good reasons for the regulations and careful adherence to them is necessary to preserve the fisheries available.

Among the regulations which most impact trout anglers are the following:

Anglers must release all Dolly Varden bull trout. Wild steelhead (rainbow trout more than 20 inches long) caught between June 1–November 30 must be released. Hatchery steelhead may be kept and are identified by a healed scar where the adipose or ventral fin has been removed.

*General Seasons.* Lakes, ponds and reservoirs: same as State of Washington Lake and Stream seasons, subject to specific exceptions stated in Olympic National Park Regulations.

*Daily Limit.* 2 trout or whitefish. There are no daily limits for eastern brook.

*Possession Limits.* No more than the equivalent of two daily limits.

Outside the Park, a Washington State License is required and regulations are established by the State. The annual regulations pamphlet and licenses are not available within Olympic National Park but are sold in most hardware and sporting goods stores on the Olympic Peninsula.

A Washington State special punchcard is necessary when fishing for steelhead and salmon, both inside and outside the Park. NOTE: All regulations are subject to annual change. Anglers must obtain current regulations.

When fishing the Olympic Mountains, use barbless hooks and practice catch and release, unless fishing for eastern brook and planning to eat them. Not only do regulations require this in nearly all waters, it is essential to sustaining the fish population.

## How to Release Fish Unharmed

1. Fish with flies or artificial lures and single barbless hooks. Never use treble hooks.
2. Leave the fish in the water.
3. Do not squeeze the fish.
4. Do not touch the gills or hold the fish by the gill covers.
5. If the fish has swallowed the hook in the gill, eye, or tongue, it should be kept if it is legal to do so. Most fish hooked in these areas will die.
6. Release the fish only after it has regained its equilibrium. If necessary, hold the fish gently and move it forward and backward to move water through its gills.

# Olympic National Park Regulations

## Hiking and Camping Regulations

Vehicles are not allowed off Park roads.

Bicycles are prohibited on all Park trails except for the Spruce Railroad Trail along Lake Crescent and the Olympic Hot Springs Trail.

Pets are prohibited on all Park trails except Rialto Beach on the coast.

Firearms are prohibited throughout the Park.

Feeding animals is prohibited.

## Wilderness Use Guidelines

*Wilderness Use Permits.* Permits are required for all overnight stays in the back country. They are free and can be obtained at all ranger stations and some trailheads.

*Campsites.* Camp only in existing campsites or those areas devoid of vegetation. Camp at least one–half mile from any trailhead and avoid camping within 100 feet of water. In some areas, camping is permitted in designated sites only. These sites will be identified by signs, markers or camp area maps. When camping avoid all areas undergoing revegetation efforts: signs, erosion matting and transplanted vegetation are evidence of this work. Avoid any recovering trails blocked with rocks, logs, branches or signs.

*Stoves.* The use of stoves is encouraged in all back country areas to minimize impact to soils and vegetation.

*Areas Closed to Open Fires.* West of the Elwha and North Fork Quinault rivers all areas above 3500 feet in elevation are closed to open fires. East of the Elwha and North Fork Quinault rivers all areas above 4000 feet in elevation are closed to open fires. In addition, there are numerous local areas closed to open fires or with limited open fires. Check with nearest ranger station.

*Latrines.* When a privy is not available, dig a shallow (4–6 inches) cat hole and cover it when finished. Locate cat holes a minimum of 100 feet from water sources. Do not locate cat holes in areas of high use, especially near camping areas. Urinate on rocks or trails.

*Refuse.* Pack out all trash. Refuse must not be placed in privies.

*Washing.* Soap and wash water should be dumped on well drained soil at least 100 feet from water sources. Minimize use of soaps, even so–called biodegradable types. Do not wash with soap in streams or rivers.

*Giardiasis.* This is an intestinal disease caused by a protozoan called giardia. Giardia is carried by humans and other animals and can contaminate water supplies. A reliable treatment for giardia is to filter, chemically treat or boil for 5 minutes.

*Group Size.* Group size limit for overnight trips is 12 individuals. Some areas have group sites, inquire at ranger station.

*Trails.* Stay on trails—avoid cutting switch backs. When encountering stock parties, stand on the downhill side of animals and converse in normal voice with rider. Stock parties have the right of way.

*Pack Stock Use.* There are park–wide and local requirements. Contact nearest ranger station for requirements.

*Food Storage.* To store food away from bears and other animals, use established poles, wires, or lockers where available. In other areas hang all food items on a line stretched between two trees so that the bags are at least 12 feet above the ground and 10 feet from the trees. Store at night and when away from camp.

*Daily Entry Quotas.* Quotas are in effect from Memorial Day to Labor Day for Lake Constance, Flapjack Lakes, Grand Valley, and the Ozette Loop. Check with nearest ranger station. In Seven Lakes Basin, camping is limited to designated sites only and permits must be obtained at Eagle Ranger Station on a first come basis.

# Olympic National Forest Wilderness Regulations

No mechanized vehicles

No campfires above 3500 feet.

Specific rules and regulations are also applicable to certain trails and areas. To obtain up–to–date information, contact Olympic National Park and

Olympic National Forest headquarters and the ranger station nearest your chosen destination.

# Useful Information

## Telephone Numbers

| | |
|---|---|
| Olympic National Park Information | (360) 452–0330 |
| Olympic National Forest Information | (360) 956–2300 |
| Washington Department of Fish & Wildlife (lake and river information outside Olympic National Park) | (360) 902–2200 |
| Washington State Ferry Information | (800) 84–FERRY |
| Airline Information—Horizon Air | (800) 547–9308 |
| Bus Information—PA–Seattle Bus Line | (360) 457–4580 |
| Clallam Transit | (360) 452–4511 |

## Entrance Fees to Olympic National Park

At the following Park entrances, small fees are charged per vehicle and per pedestrian: Elwha, Hurricane Ridge, Hoh, Sol Duc and Staircase entrances. All other access is without charge.

## Weather

Spring is cool and often wet, high temperatures in the upper 50's and 60's at lower elevations and much colder at high elevations. Most of the high elevation areas remain snowed in until at least early summer. Summer high temperatures average in the low 70's, cooling 20–30 degrees and more at night. Summer is generally much drier, but heavy clothing and rain gear should always be available. Temperatures drop in the Fall, and rain becomes more frequent, but much of the season is dry. The Olympics receive the vast majority of precipitation in Winter, when daytime temperatures average in the low 40's.

## Lodging

Olympic National Park has lodging available on the West Side at Klaloch Lodge, (360) 962–2271 and Lake Quinault Lodge, (360) 288–2900; on the North Side at Sol Duc Hot Springs Resort, (360) 327–3583, Lake Crescent Lodge, (360) 928–3211, and Log Cabin Resort (Lake Crescent) (360) 928–3245.

There are numerous motels in the towns surrounding the Olympic Mountains.

## Ranger Stations

Specific information about each area of the National Forest and National Park can be obtained at the various Ranger Stations.

*North.* ONP– ONP Headquarters, 600 East Park Ave, Port Angeles, WA, 98362, (360) 452–4501; Lake Crescent Ranger Station, HC62, Box 10, Port Angeles, WA, 98331, (360) 928–3380. ONF/ ONP–Sol Duc Ranger Station, Route 1, Box 5750, Forks, WA, 98331, (360) 374–6522

*West.* ONP–Hoh Ranger Station, HC80, Box 650, Forks, WA, 98331, (360) 962–2283; Mora Ranger Station, HC79, Box 170, Forks WA, 98331, (360)374–5460. ONF–Quinault Ranger Station, Rt.1, Box 9, Quinault, WA, 98575, (360) 288–2525

*East.* ONF/ONP– Hood Canal Ranger Station, P.O. Box 68, Hoodsport, WA, 98548, (360) 877–5254. ONF–Quilcene Ranger Station, P.O. Box 280, Quilcene, WA, 98376, (360) 765–3368.

## Fly Fishing Shops

Quality Fly Fishing Shop, 2720 E. Highway 101, Port Angeles, WA,
(360) 452–5942

The Northwest Angler, 18830 Front St. Poulsbo, WA, (360) 697–7100

The Fly Fisher, 5622 Pacific Ave SE, Lacey, WA, (360) 491–0181

The Backcast, 720 Simpson, Hoquiam, WA, (360) 532–6867

Olympic Sporting Goods, Almar Bldg., Forks, WA, (360) 374–6330

## Fishing Tackle–General

Swain's General Store, 602 E. First, Port Angeles, WA, (360) 452–2357

Tri–Area Sporting Goods, 10962 Rhody Dr., Port Hadlock, WA, (360)
385–4069

Winslow Hardware, 240 Winslow Way E. Bainbridge, WA, (206) 842–
3101

Archers and Anglers, 401 Creek St. Yelm, WA, (360) 458–5093

Big 5 Sporting Goods, 909 Cooper Point Rd. SW, Olympia, WA, (360)
786 6529

Puget Sound Sports Center, 527 Devoe S.W., Olympia, WA, (360) 943–
4867

Tumwater Sports Center, 6200 Capitol Blvd. SE, Tumwater, WA, (360)
352–5161

All Season Sports, 815 1/2 Simpson, Hoquiam, WA, (360) 538–7033

Amanda Park Mercantile, 6088 Highway 10l, Amanda Park, WA, (360)
288–2564

Big Mouth John's, 521 E. 1st, Aberdeen, WA, (360) 533–0143

Belfair Hardware, Belfair, WA, (360) 275–2031

Kitsap Sports, Clear Creek Center, Silverdale, WA, (360) 698–4808

# Topographic Maps and Guidebooks

Hiking Guidebooks and topographic maps are a necessity, not an option, in most cases for anglers fishing the Olympic Mountains.

## Hiking Guidebooks

*Olympic Mountains Trail Guide*, Robert Wood, The Mountaineers, Seattle,
Washington, 1985.

*Climber's Guide to the Olympic Mountains*, Olympic Mountain Rescue, The
    Mountaineers, Seattle, Washington, 1988.
*The Trail Guide to Olympic National Park*, Erik Molvar, Falcon Press,
    Helena, Montana, 1995.

## Topographic Maps

*Custom Correct Topographic Maps*, Little River Enterprises, 3492 Little
    River Road, Port Angeles, Washington, 98363.
*Green Trails*, PO Box 1272, Bellevue, Washington, 98009.

# Campgrounds

## Western Olympics

### Bogachiel

Bogachiel State Park: 6 miles south of Forks on Highway 101, 36 sites,
    water, fee.

### Hoh

Hoh Oxbow: on the Hoh River 4 miles south of Forks, 5 sites, no water,
    no fee.

Cottonwood: on the Hoh River 15 miles south of Forks, 6 sites, water,
    no fee.

Wiloughby Creek: Bert Cole State Forest, 14 miles south of Forks on
    Highway 101, 3.5 miles on Hoh Rain Forest Road, 3 sites, no water,
    no fee.

Minnie Peterson: on the Hoh River 1 mile past Willoughby Creek
    Campground, 6 sites, water, no fee.

Hoh Rainforest: ONP, at the end of the Hoh River Road, 89 sites, water,
    fee.

South Fork Hoh: Bert Cole State Forest, 15 miles south of Forks, east on
    Hoh Road, left on H1000 road 7.5 miles, 3 sites. no water, no fee.

### Quinault

July Creek: on north shore of Lake Quinault, walk–in only, 29 sites,
    water, no fee.

Willaby: on Lake Quinault, 2 sites, water, fee. Falls Creek, on Lake
    Quinault, 8 sites, water, no fee.

Gatton Creek: on Lake Quinault, 13 sites, water, fee.

Graves Creek: 15 miles on Quinault Road, 30 sites, no fee.

### Queets

Queets Campground: 14 miles on Queets Road, 20 sites, no water, no fee.

## Southern Olympics

### Wynoochee

Coho: on Wynoochee Lake, 8 sites, water, fee

*South Fork Skokomish.*
> Brown Creek: on S. Fork Skokomish River, 22 sites, water, fee.

# Northern Olympics

*Dungeness*
> Dungeness Forks: on the Dungeness River, 7 miles from Highway 101, 9 sites, water, fee.
> East Crossing: 2–3 miles beyond Dungeness Forks Campground, 9 sites, water, fee.

*Deer Park*
> Deer Park: at the end of Deer Park Road, 18 miles from Highway 101, 18 sites, water. no fee.

*Hurricane Ridge*
> Heart O' the Hills: 5 miles on Hurricane Ridge Road, 105 sites, water, fee.

*Elwha*
> Altaire: on the Lower Elwha River, 30 sites, water, fee. Elwha, on the Lower Elwha River, 41 sites, water, fee.

*Sol Duc*
> Klahowya: on the Sol Duc River 101 20 miles northeast of Forks, 49 sites, water, fee.
> Sol Duc: on the Sol Duc River 12 miles from Highway 101 on Sol Duc road, 80 sites, water, fee.

*Lake Crescent*
> Fairholm: on Lake Crescent, 87 sites, fee.

# Eastern Olympics

*Quilcene*
> Falls View: above Quilcene River on Highway 101 4 miles south of Quilcene, 35 sites, water, fee.
> Rainbow: 2 miles south of Falls View on Highway 101, 9 sites, no water, no fee.

*Dosewallips*
> Dosewallips State Park: on Hood Canal 1 mile south of Brinnon, 127 sites, water, fee.
> Elkhorn: 10 miles on Dosewallips Road, 18 sites, water, fee.
> Dosewallips: at the end of the Dosewallips Road, 30 sites, water, no fee.

*Duckabush*
> Camp Collins: 7 miles on Duckabush Road, 14 sites, water, fee.

*Hamma Hamma*
> Hamma Hamma: 7 miles on Hamma Hamma Road, 15 sites, water, fee.
> Lena Creek: 4 miles past Hamma Hamma Campground, 14 sites, water, fee.

*Lake Cushman/ North Fork Skokomish*
> Lake Cushman State Park: on Lake Cushman, 81 sites, water, fee.

Big Creek: 2 miles past Lake Cushman State Park, 23 sites, water, fee.
Staircase: end of Lake Cushman Road, 17 miles from Highway 101, 59
sites, water, fee.

# *Sources*

Hagen, H. K. Draft *Visitor' Fishing Guide, Olympic National Park*, unpublished, 1961.

Hagen, H. K. *An inceptive study of the distribution and relative condition of
the endemic and exotic fishes of several selected areas in Olympic
National Park,* unpublished, 1961.

Johnston, James. *High Lake and Stream Survey Report Olympic National
Forest –Parts I and II,* Washington State Game Dept., 1972–73.

Jones, Stan. *Washington State Fishing Guide*, Stan Jones Publishing Inc.,
Seattle, Washington. Seventh Edition, 1995.

Houston, D. B., Research Biologist Pacific Northwest Region. *Anadromous
Fish in Olympic National Park: A Status Report*, National Park Service,
1983.

Molvar, Erik. *The Trail Guide to Olympic National Park.*, Falcon Press
Publishing Co., Helena, Montana, 1995.

Olson, Richard and Meyer, John, Natural Resources Managment Division
Olympic National Park, Port Angeles, Washington *Survey of Non–Native
Fish in Selected Interior Lakes of Olympic National Park,* 1992–1994.

Olympic Mountain Rescue. *Climbers Guide to the Olympic Mountains*, The
Mountaineers, Seattle, Washington, 1988.

Parrat, Smitty. *Gods & Goblins, A field Guide to Place Names of the Olympic National Park*, 1984.

Stienstra, Tom. *Pacific Northwest Camping Guide*, Foghorn Press, San
Francisco, California, 1994.

Walker, Wendy. *The Recreation Guide to Washington National Forests*,
Falcon Press Publishing Co., Helena, Montana, 1993.

Washington Writer's Program, WPA Washington. *Guide to the Evergreen
State,* Metropolitan Press, Portland, Oregon, 1941.

Webster, E.B. *Fishing in the Olympics*, The Evening News Inc., Port Angeles, Washington, 1923.

Wolcott, Ernest E. *Lakes of Washington,* Dept. of Conservation Water
Supply Bulletin Western Washington Edition, 1964.

Wood, Robert. *Olympic Mountains Trail Guide*, The Mountaineers, Seattle,
Washington, 1984.

# Index